Lead The Way

How To Change The World From A Teen Activist And School Striker

Jean Hinchliffe

16pt

Copyright Page from the Original Book

PANTERA PRESS

The information in this book is published in good faith and for general information purposes only. Although the author and publisher believe at the time of going to press that the information is correct, they do not assume and hereby disclaim any liability to any party for any loss, damage or disruption caused by errors or omissions, whether they result from negligence, accident or any other cause.

First published in 2021 by Pantera Press Pty Limited
www.PanteraPress.com

Text Copyright © Jean Hinchliffe, 2021
Copyright © Illustration Astred Hicks, Design Cherry

Jean Hinchliffe has asserted her moral rights to be identified as the author of this work.
Design and Typography Copyright © Pantera Press Pty Limited, 2021
® Pantera Press, three-slashes colophon device, and *sparking imagination, conversation* & *change* are registered trademarks of Pantera Press Pty Limited. Lost the Plot is a trademark of Pantera Press Pty Limited

This work is copyright, and all rights are reserved. Apart from any use permitted under *Copyright legislation*, no part may be reproduced or transmitted in any form or by any means, nor may any other exclusive right be exercised, without the publisher's prior permission in writing. We welcome your support of the author's rights, so please only buy authorised editions.

Please send all permission queries to:
Pantera Press, P.O. Box 1989, Neutral Bay, NSW 2089, Australia or info@PanteraPress.com

A Cataloguing-in-Publication entry for this book is available from the National Library of Australia.

Cover design and internal illustrations: Astred Hicks, Design Cherry
Author photo: Graham Jepson
Publisher: Lex Hirst
Editor: Jane Price
Proofreaders: Kirsty van der Veer and Lucy Bell
Typesetting: Kirby Jones
Printed in Australia by McPherson's Printing Group

TABLE OF CONTENTS

INTRODUCTION	i
PART ONE: An urge to fight for what's right	1
CHAPTER 1: DECIDING TO DO SOMETHING	3
CHAPTER 2: UNDERSTANDING CHANGE	8
CHAPTER 3: TAKING YOUR FIRST STEPS	21
PART TWO: The activist toolkit	72
CHAPTER 4: LOBBYING POLITICIANS	74
CHAPTER 5: THE ULTIMATE GUIDE TO HOLDING A PROTEST	93
PART THREE: Powering your movement	150
CHAPTER 6: PROMOTION – THE ART OF REACHING PEOPLE	152
CHAPTER 7: HOW TO WRITE GREAT EMAILS	159
CHAPTER 8: SOCIAL MEDIA – MAKE IT WORK FOR YOU	162
CHAPTER 9: THE POWER OF MAINSTREAM MEDIA	167
CHAPTER 10: PUBLIC SPEAKING	180
CHAPTER 11: COMMUNICATION WITHIN THE TEAM	192
CHAPTER 12: TIME MANAGEMENT	204
CHAPTER 13: LONGEVITY: TAKING CARE OF YOURSELF AND EACH OTHER	210
CONCLUSION: LOOKING BACK AND LOOKING AHEAD	231
ACKNOWLEDGEMENTS	234

INTRODUCTION

HEY! I'M JEAN, AND I'M A YOUTH ACTIVIST, WITH CLIMATE justice being my current primary focus. As you've made the decision to pick up this book, I assume you too have a strong desire to make the world a better place. And, honestly, that's all you need to become completely and utterly absorbed into the world of change-making. This universe is, at points, chaotic and daunting, yet it's always an invigorating and beautiful space where people from all walks of life band together to fight for what's right. Becoming an activist has been one of the most rewarding aspects of my life, and I hope this guide helps you navigate that same journey. Before we jump in, I thought I'd share my 'activist story' – how I became so deeply involved in activism so quickly, and why it's become such an important part of my life.

I've always been a pretty political and loud-mouthed kid. I became a passionate debater and public speaker at the ripe old age of eight, thanks to my Year Three teacher, Mr Dodds. There was something thrilling about getting up on stage and attempting to demolish the other team's arguments – even on such typically exciting school-mandated topics as 'Should the canteen be allowed to sell sugary foods?' and 'Should sport be mandatory?' However, we also debated some more interesting motions, such as whether we should continue to celebrate Australia Day, or if gambling should be made illegal. These programs are in many ways what first allowed me to raise my voice, teaching me the value of speaking up.

Although my family is quite progressive, they've never been the sort to join local action groups or become heavily involved in campaigning. Because of this, the first rally I ever attended was the 2017 Women's March in Sydney. I hadn't actually realised it was happening that day, and discovered its existence when a friend invited me to come along with her family. When we rocked up to Hyde Park a few minutes after the rally had officially begun, I was completely gobsmacked at the crowds of people flooding through the grounds. About 5000 people were crammed into the area, a sea of pink pussyhats and hand-painted banners. I thought it was the most incredible thing I'd ever seen. We chanted as we marched through the city: cries of feminism, girl power and intersectionality. I'd never felt an energy like that before; it was entirely consuming, both electrifying and seemingly endless. I knew in that moment that I wanted the feeling to last long after the march.

Towards the end of that year, the marriage equality plebiscite was held. After months of tireless debate, the voluntary postal survey was called by the federal government. It asked a simple question: should the law be changed to allow same-sex couples to marry? But the public response was anything but simple. It put all LGBTQ+ people on the chopping block, threatening their identities and livelihoods while loud political and media voices likened same-sex marriage to bestiality, paedophilia and polygamy. The hatred and attacks against the community were awful, leading to measurable impacts on the wellbeing of many queer people. I was incredibly frustrated by the whole situation, but had no clue how to help. Then one night I saw a tweet from the YES campaign, recruiting volunteers for phone banking. I clicked through to the website and immediately signed up. One of my mother's conditions for letting me go along to a meeting of random adults in an office building in the city at 7.30pm was (quite reasonably) that I had to take a friend. I gave my mate Marley a call and, luckily for me, she was keen to help.

Dressed in our sweaty school sports uniforms, we made our way into the YES campaign HQ. It was very nearly an average office space, but the rainbow flags covering every available wall ruined its chances of looking at all ordinary. As we took our seats, it became clear that we were the youngest people in the room by about twenty years. We slunk into our little corner, trying to act as if this were a totally normal situation and we didn't feel wildly awkward. We were separated into small groups and went through a few icebreaker introductions, explaining how we had come to volunteer. It was interesting to see that the majority of people there didn't actually identify as queer, but had still taken time out of their evenings to support a cause that didn't directly impact them. Then we started our training. We were supplied with a script that worked as a flowchart to guide the conversation. The goal of the calls was that if the person was in support of marriage equality, we would get them to pledge to send in their vote as soon as they received the ballot. And, if they had already received the ballot, they would send it in immediately after we finished the call.

It was simple work, but I was unusually nervous. I guess cold-calling strangers to ask about their personal and political beliefs is just a little anxiety-inducing. But pretty quickly I managed to summon up the guts to start dialling. After navigating the robot voice system, we were placed in the 'call queue' and spent time listening to the on-hold music. Because this was a marriage-equality campaign, I was anticipating some classic queer hits. The music was most certainly classic, but not of that variety: we were confronted with a disconcertingly dramatic and gothic orchestral song that would jarringly cut out every time we were connected to a call. Most people who were picking up the phone automatically assumed I was an adult; I don't think I've been referred to as 'ma'am' in any other situation. Happily, most callers were incredibly sweet and willing to talk. The worst interactions I had were with very gruff-sounding men telling me that they simply did not want to discuss this over the phone.

By the end of the evening I didn't even need to look at the script anymore; I had recited it so many times it had become muscle memory. It was a surprisingly exhausting task and I couldn't wait to get to bed. But it was also remarkably empowering and rewarding.

> **EVEN THOUGH I WASN'T OLD ENOUGH TO VOTE OR OFFICIALLY CHANGE THE SITUATION, I FELT AS THOUGH I WAS MAKING A TANGIBLE DIFFERENCE.**

After that, I volunteered at the phone bank several times each week. A little later in the campaign, I put up my hand to deliver flyers and stick up posters in my neighbourhood. As, by then, I was a pretty involved volunteer, I was given about four times the usual amount of materials to hand out, so I called my friend Phoebe and together we spent our entire Saturday afternoon putting them up (after a rather slow start – Phoebe was knitting on the bus and missed her stop twice). It was a laborious process but, with great effort, we managed to tape up about 300 posters between us. Once they were all up, we stood outside Woolworths and handed out the leftover flyers. One encouraging aspect of this process was the volume of people who rejected our material because they had already sent in their 'yes' votes.

Over the next year, I spent time getting involved with a heap of different campaigns, although I never really took on a leadership position or totally dived into it. I worked mostly with the #StopAdani campaign and my local GetUp group. Then, in early October, I started to see enormous amounts of news coverage of a new United Nations report, which had given the world a deadline of twelve years to avert the worst impacts of the climate crisis. I felt as if a fire had been lit underneath me and more than anything I needed to act. I signed up to every environmental non-government organisation I could find and started researching ways in which I could get active. It was frustrating to see that almost every program and group seemed very adult-centric and didn't really make space for young people – even though I wanted to do as much as I could, I couldn't figure out how. A week or so later, at about midnight (on a school night!), my friend Louise sent me a link to the newly formed School Strike 4 Climate (SS4C) website. At that point, climate striking was a totally novel and revolutionary concept. Greta Thunberg had received a little attention and gained an online following but was nowhere near the household name she is today. Yet I knew from the moment I opened the website that I had to take part. I scrolled through to find the Sydney event details but the only strike listed was in Melbourne. As a passionate and frustrated sleep-deprived teenager, I decided to immediately send an email explaining how I would love to help out if an event was being organised in Sydney.

I woke up in the morning to a very enthusiastic response. I remember reading through the reply email and seeing the line, 'We'd love to help you achieve this goal'. Crap. I hadn't quite intended to put up my hand to make it all happen, let alone state that the strike was my goal. It felt like an awfully large responsibility placed on very underqualified shoulders. As I was grabbing breakfast before leaving for school, I briefly mentioned the concept to my mum.

'Jeez,' she said, 'can't they get any adults to do it?'

I arrived at school that morning and began to tell my friends about this new project I had signed up for, not entirely believing what I was saying. As I explained the concept of the strike, I made sure to throw in bucket-loads of 'maybes' and 'potentiallys' in an effort not to promise something I was unsure would even happen. Most people seemed interested, though I don't think anyone viewed the idea with the same level of excitement I did. Whether or not I possessed the skills to pull it off, I knew deep inside that the strike could have the power to really change things.

That evening, I started brainstorming locations for the strike, and plotting how exactly I could get Millie Bobby Brown to shout us out on Instagram. I made a brief document as I continued planning, which included the fantastic line: 'Overall message should be "stop shitting on our futures".'

Thankfully, it was in no way a solo effort. Word of the strike began to spread, and over the next few weeks our group grew from a couple of students and adult supporters into a proper team with heaps of volunteers. Everyone put in hours of work, sending letters to politicians, booking speaker systems and organising 'crafternoons'. It was an insane process. No one had official roles or responsibilities; rather, we all just put up our hands for anything we had the capacity to do.

A couple of weeks before the strike, I had my first ever TV interview, with *The Feed* on SBS. I received the call at school and leapt at the opportunity to get the word out. The offices were slick and professional: I tried to soak up everything around me, to fully comprehend all the excitement. I was led into a little room for hair and makeup before entering the studio space. It was exactly like those news tables you see on TV, although I'd never noticed just how big they are. The hosts were in a different studio to me and, as all the cameras were remotely operated, after my mic was put on I was the only person in the room. It was enormously intimidating, but I ended up enjoying myself immensely. The hosts were cracking jokes throughout, while at the same time discussing the movement with a clear tone of sincerity. As I sat there, it struck me how strange the entire situation was. I was essentially a random kid, and by some stroke of luck had found myself dazed by studio lights in front of a massive camera, talking about a project which I had been involved in for less than a fortnight. It was then I realised that I wasn't spending time creating some random intangible thing; I was part of something that was undeniably present. Being in that situation made everything feel significantly more real.

After an exhausting month, the day of the first strike arrived. Now, I've got to say, I was terrified. Part of organising large-scale events is not knowing what the turnout will be. I remember thinking to myself: *If we do well, about 500 kids will show up; if we totally crush it, then maybe there will be a thousand.*

Over an hour before the strike was due to start, I arrived at Martin Place with a swarm of students from my school. I was surprised to see that people were already showing up; small clumps of colour scattered through the space as students hovered in groups of school friends. We hadn't completely considered the logistics of where we wanted to be in the space, leading to us setting up half our speaker system in one spot before frantically carrying it back down again after realising that a fountain feature at the other end had a flat elevated area that functioned perfectly as a stage. About fifteen minutes before the strike was set to start, I was being interviewed just off the side of the stage. I was facing away from the crowd but could still see everyone coming in. It was incredible: a constant and seemingly endless stream of people. When I turned around again at the end of the interview, I was stunned. The whole area was filled to the brim, and there were still ten minutes to go. More and more people came crowding in. I vividly remember what appeared to be an entire year group from a private girls' school all arriving at once, each student decked out in a bright blue dress and holding a handpainted sign.

Speaking in front of all these people was the most terrifying and exhilarating moment of my life. I felt tears begin to well as I looked across the crowd. It was chaos – a sea of thousands of different uniforms and posters and cheers. I tentatively approached the microphone, gripping the cool metal in my sweaty palms. I took a deep breath, and somehow managed to quash my nerves enough to begin talking. It took me a moment to adjust to speaking through the microphone; I initially stumbled over words as I heard the unfamiliar echo of my voice, though I quickly found my rhythm and my confidence grew. I knew as I wrote my speech that I wanted one message to ring clearest of all:

> **THAT YOUNG PEOPLE WERE SICK AND TIRED OF OUR FUTURES BEING DESTROYED.**

And we were going to fight as hard as we could to force those in charge to take immediate climate action.

After every line I spoke, the crowd would respond with a deafening cheer. I remember this sounding loudest of all as I cried that this was just our first action, just our first step to achieving this dream. Although I didn't realise it at the time, if I watch footage of myself from that day I notice how every time I finish a line I hold a serious activist-y face for a second, before breaking into the hugest smile you can imagine. I'm sure I've never smiled so much in my life. I just couldn't believe that so many people would come together for something I'd helped make possible, that we'd sparked a movement so much bigger than ourselves. The whole event carried an electricity that is difficult to describe: it's as if we had bottled up all the anger and frustration from years of never being listened to and released it into the square, transforming it into a place of hope and undeniable power. Despite being a movement that was so new and fresh, we pulled together young people in a way that no one had thought possible.

A total of 5000 students turned out that day – a number that continues to amaze me. The event was a beautiful collection of speakers and musicians, from my co-host, Manjot Kaur, who spoke with such ferocity and passion, to a group of Pacific Climate Warriors, who finished with a chant of 'We're not drowning, we are fighting!', to Lucie Atkin-Bolton, an eleven-year-old primary school student, who delivered a clear-cutting about our need for climate action, and the ARIA-award-winning artist Montaigne, who is incredibly outspoken about the climate crisis, to name a few.

It was strange to walk past Martin Place later that day. Although it looked the same as always – dotted with business people on their lunch breaks and a stream of commuters entering and exiting the train station – it felt as though something was missing.

The two years or so since that first strike have been a whirlwind. We've staged another two major strikes, both on globally shared dates – 15 March and 20 September 2019. March was the first event to which we extended the invitation to adults so they could attend in solidarity. As always, I was terrified that no one would show up; however, our turnout increased tenfold, to 150,000 nationally. We held our first ever general strike on 20 September, as part of the global climate strike. We worked with churches, unions, community groups, businesses and many more to pull together Australia's largest ever climate mobilisation. Over 1.3 per cent of the population joined us that day, the event galvanising around 350,000 people in over 100 locations. Despite the COVID-19 crisis throwing a major wrench in our plans, we've still found ways to continue taking action. On 15 May 2020, we staged our first digital action as a movement. It involved a four-hour nationally broadcast livestream, packed full of panel conversations, musical performances, speeches, and interactive elements. Though it was pulled together at the last minute and unlike anything we had tried in the past, about 50,000 people tuned in to the livestream. I was in shock; against all odds we had still found a way to make our voices heard. Later, on 25 September, we staged a day of action against the federal government's proposed gas-led recovery. We directly collaborated with unions and First-Nations groups, to amplify voices of those most impacted by the issue. Anyone was able to stage an action under the SS4C banner (provided they did so in a COVID-safe manner), resulting in a diverse range of online and in-person protests, including digital rallies, massive fabric letters spelling 'FUND OUR FUTURE' laid in a park in Brisbane, and a bright-yellow barge sailing in front of the Sydney Opera House, to name a few. Over 600 actions were organised for the day, making for the biggest ever national protest against gas.

Since our inception, we've grown so much as a movement, both internally and in numbers, becoming a close-knit family of young people fighting for what we see as most important. It's sometimes difficult to believe now that we began with just a few schoolkids who felt a spark of inspiration and a need to take action.

> **SOMETHING I'M REALLY PASSIONATE ABOUT IS THE POWER OF COMMITTING AND SIMPLY SAYING YES.**

I spend a lot of time having conversations with other kids my age about activism and the issues that matter most to us, which consistently end with this wonderful sense of empowerment and awe at the sheer level of intelligence and ideas coming from teens. But, apart from posting on social media or attending protests and rallies, very few seem to actually act on these passions. As young people, we're often told that we're too inexperienced to make a difference, or that we're apathetic and ignorant and our voices shouldn't be listened to. Hearing this all the time makes a lot of us feel scared to take a role in activism; it seems as if those positions are reserved for people who are older, smarter and already wealthy in experience. It can be difficult to break away from these preconceived notions, but you mustn't let close-minded views limit what you're capable of.

When I first became involved in SS4C, I had absolutely no idea what I was doing. I was suddenly thrown into a new world of hour-long online meetings, formal emailing, police negotiating and strategy planning. I was constantly scrambling to figure everything out; it felt as though every passing minute brought a new challenge I had to face. It was all so different, and a lot of time it was pretty overwhelming. And, while I wouldn't have admitted it at the time, I'm now happy to state that I was incredibly underqualified for the role. (In fact, almost all of us were!) I've had to reach out for help time and time again, I've had to reach out for help time and time again, have felt utterly confused and lost sometimes, and asked countless questions along the way. I've evolved so much as an activist and person, and I'm now so proud of what I have accomplished.

As I look back on the whole experience, I can pinpoint the moments when I first decided to become involved: when I was introduced to activism through volunteering with the YES campaign; when I decided to continue working with other groups; and when I dived in headfirst and joined SS4C. These were the times when I simply committed, putting up my hand for something that was way out my comfort zone. If I had let the doubt others had in me, or even my own fears, get in the way, I would have totally missed out on this life-changing experience.

I would never have met all the profoundly passionate and kind people I work with every day, never have gained the experience that continues to make me feel confident in my own abilities.

Most importantly, I would've prevented myself from making a real difference.

If you feel passion about something and an urge to fight for what's right, I can't encourage you enough to take a leap of faith. You might be afraid that you're too small to change anything, or that you'll be put in a situation way out of your comfort zone and not be able to cope. It's okay to be scared – it's a natural reaction – but it's vital you don't stop your journey there.

> **AT THE END OF THE DAY, IF YOU DON'T TAKE ACTION, THEN WHO WILL?**

It took me a long time to feel comfortable using the word 'activist'. It seems like such an official term, and if I picked it up too early or used it too comfortably I felt I'd be seen as a fraud. The truth of it is, however, that anyone who gets involved in campaigning for political or social change is an activist. It's quite odd because – unlike becoming a lawyer, for example – there's no quantifiable point at which you become an activist. You don't train for the job and pass a variety of exams until someone chooses to hire you; you make the choice one day and just continue with it. It isn't a term you need to shy away from; it's something to embrace with open arms. This is an awesome space to be involved in, and you deserve to recognise yourself for the work you do.

This book is an amalgamation of practical advice and personal stories from my time as an organiser. It's a collection of everything I've learnt over the past few years. Remember, when you're reading, that there really is no right or wrong way to make change; everyone goes on this journey at their own pace. As you become part of this amazing community, I hope you find yourself coming back to this guide and gaining insights from it, and taking comfort in knowing that you are not alone – and that together, we can change the world.

1

PART ONE

An urge to fight for what's right

When you look at the magnitude of the issues we face today, it's hard to find the motivation to go out and try to change things: it can seem as though the problems out there are so deeply ingrained that it's simply impossible to make a difference. That feeling of hopelessness is one of the major reasons so many people don't allow themselves to try to create change.

But letting yourself hide under the covers is doing nobody any favours. The world can be a strange and scary place, and it's everyone's duty to brighten it up, even just a little. Though you might feel insignificant, the biggest changes always come from the accumulation of tiny actions. Don't allow yourself to stay silent; only through taking a stand can you realise how much power you hold. Every person who makes the choice to dive into the deep end is part of the solution to transforming how our world works.

2

CHAPTER I

DECIDING TO DO SOMETHING

IT CAN OFTEN SEEM AS IF THE WORLD IS RIDDLED WITH injustice. It's impossible to watch the news or open Instagram without being bombarded with information about the many deeply unfair situations taking place today. It's a lot to comprehend: much more than the average person can take in. As you're flooded with all this information, it's hard not to become numb to everything – a symptom of the complete overwhelm at the world we're all faced with.

Like many others, I've spent a great deal of time trying to understand exactly how we landed in the variety of messes we're in today. For quite a while, I assumed that all the problems must be completely separate in causation; that such omnipresent prejudice and hatred was all some sick coincidence. It was a baffling thing to consider: that somehow society institutionally continued to see those who were 'other' as different and lesser, and that that group encompassed so many people. Because all these issues were about such different things, I was sure that while they were united by hatred and a disregard for others, the hatred was all somehow separate. That although, say, racism and sexism both stem from a belief that white people or cisgender men are inherently superior, they still inhabit entirely separate spaces. So I was sure that they needed to be fought as separate issues, and that somehow we'd have to find ways to individually work through each one from the ground up.

It took some time, but slowly my perspective began to shift. I remember the biggest 'aha' moment I had was during a walk alone through a park. I'd been marching along for quite some time and my mind (as it often does) was running off in countless directions. I began to think about the climate strikes and how, despite the numbers of people we'd been able to mobilise, it felt that real change was still a long, long way away. It's a thought that still comes to me frequently, typically accompanied by a brief stint of existential dread, but this time I started going through a different thought process. Because although many people and politicians still denied the climate crisis, polling had recently shown that a good majority of the Australian public believed in climate change and thought we needed to take action on it. It seemed so strange, then, that absolutely nothing was being done about it.

Industries were still polluting enormously, governments weren't investing in renewable energy or implementing any meaningful climate policy, and it looked as if it was going to be another year in which the issue was swept under the rug.

But what seemed strangest of all was that this made no logical sense. Sure, there were some short-term economic benefits to continuing these behaviours that fuelled the climate crisis, but ultimately, within about 10 years, they'd be completely fruitless and we'd be in a far worse off position. And, looking beyond economics, we were staring into the face of the largest crisis humanity has ever faced – literal, predictable and preventable doom. And yet, everyone in power was sticking their heads in the sand. This crisis was going to cause a lot more than a slightly hotter summer: it was going to create food insecurity, job losses, massive natural disasters, increased poverty and disease, and would worsen all other social issues in the process. The fact that we existed in such a state of denial to a crisis that we had caused made, and still makes, zero sense. I think it was this awareness of the sheer absurdity of the situation that prompted me to think a bit more critically about our society as a whole.

> **I REALISED IN THAT MOMENT THAT SOMETHING WAS DEEPLY, DEEPLY WRONG IN THE WAY THAT WE EXIST. AND IT WAS ALL ROOTED IN POWER.**

Somehow, power has been distributed across our society in a way that is to the detriment of the broader community. There's no way that a truly fair and democratic world could fall into such a position of rapid impending doom, yet that is exactly where we have landed. Not only has the climate crisis been *caused* by this inequity, but all other existing social issues have been too. As long as power isn't distributed fairly – in a way that allows civil society to have a voice and speak up – we'll be trapped forever in a cycle of injustice.

I look back on the ways I used to think and I can't help noticing how naive I was. I was very young and had an oversimplified view of the world; but, by the same token, who was there to tell me otherwise? It's only natural to take inequality and social difficulties at a purely surface level. Understanding the links between these issues is difficult; further attempting to realise the bigger problems that lie beneath the surface and hold them up is even more so. But, if we don't recognise the issues with how power is distributed, we can't ever make true and lasting progress. If these base issues and structures continue to exist as they currently do, even as we solve some issues of inequality, more and more problems will arise.

CHAPTER 2
UNDERSTANDING CHANGE

SOMETHING THAT I FIND QUITE BEAUTIFUL ABOUT ACTIVISM is the way successful movements throughout history are all so similar once they're stripped down. We continue to use different strategies and tactics, but the roots of how to best make change are all very much interlinked. You'll often find that one of the most inspirational and helpful resources for developing strategy is to explore the methodologies, successes and shortcomings of past movements. Despite taking place in vastly different contexts, the flames of social change throughout history have great parallels. Not only are these movements wonderful to learn from, but their activists have left us a plethora of written information about their own personal theories of change and experiences in activism. In this information are the many deeply apparent parallels, clear paths and techniques that enabled great change to be made in the past, from the Indigenous civil rights movement of the 1960s to the current Bla(c)k Lives Matter movement.

Activists of all forms are in many ways in sync; despite all following our own paths and discovering different ways of making change, we all march to the beat of the same drum.

> **TO BUILD EFFECTIVE SOCIAL MOVEMENTS WE NEED TO LEARN FROM THE PAST AND DEVELOP NEW TECHNIQUES FOR THE FUTURE.**

Having an understanding of theory can elevate activist groups and actions from 'just another protest' into long-lasting and transformative changes.

This section explores the theory that has informed my organising. I have been helped in writing the rest of this chapter by a mentor and friend of mine, Amanda Tattersall, an activist and academic working at the Sydney University Policy Lab.

Change yourself, or change the system?

Often people say to me: 'I prefer to do my own thing. Going on marches and all that stuff isn't for me.' While I respect everyone's right to choose for themselves, there are a few matters to raise here.

A key point in the discussion of a whole variety of social issues is the value of 'individual change' versus 'systemic change'. This conversation applies in many sectors but it is particularly relevant in the climate space. 'Individual change' is a form of change in which the responsibility is placed on the individual. An example of this would be the zero-waste movement, which pushes for people to dramatically reduce the amount of waste they produce by substituting reusable items for single-use plastics and generally shifting their lifestyle to be more eco-conscious. This can have a large effect as more and more people recognise this responsibility and adjust their behaviour, thought processes and attitudes. However, it's also possible to find fault in there being such pressure on the individual, and to argue that individuals changing their lifestyles ultimately isn't the solution we need. This argument aligns more with the concept of 'systemic change' – the belief that blame should be placed on the governments, corporations and leadership systems that have failed us, and that contribute most to these problems. It's a belief that outlines our need to change the systems surrounding us that cause the issues and lead, in turn, to individuals further perpetuating them.

While I would never dismiss the need for individual change, I personally believe that systemic change is almost always more important, and that's what this guide covers. People can't change their individual behaviour unless the systems surrounding them adapt and make it a genuinely accessible course of action. I feel that this is particularly applicable to the climate crisis, as the biggest polluters are enormously wealthy corporations and governments. In fact, since 1988 just 100 companies have been the source of more than 70 per cent of the world's greenhouse gas emissions, according to a 2018 study. Placing the blame on individuals by telling the average person that the climate crisis is their fault because they occasionally drive to school or haven't turned vegan feels in many ways like a distraction from the main issue. However, in saying this, it's also important to recognise that both methods of change are co-dependent and, while we place more emphasis on one, we can't completely ignore the other.

What is power?

I've already mentioned that the unequal distribution of power is at the root of most — if not all — injustice in society. The concept of power itself can be difficult to understand. It's an intangible construct, yet it has complete influence over our day-to-day lives.

Power isn't as simple as whoever is currently in an elected position; in fact, it's a far more subtle and somewhat abstract thing. Probably the most iconic image would be that of political power: a politician signing a document into law, or looking into the barrel of a TV camera. While this is certainly still accurate, power can also present itself in a variety of other ways. When simplified, power is essentially control over three major issues: who makes the decisions, who sets the agenda, and who sets the culture. This is the case on any scale, from deeply local to completely global. By holding power, people can disrupt how society functions, be that for the better or worse.

At its very root, activism is about recognising when power seems unfairly distributed and unjustly used, and figuring out how best to shift power to those who will make a more equitable and fair society.

The public arena

The 'public arena' is a way to describe how current society looks and how it functions. This is in reference to decision-making, culture, influence and pretty much anything else that shapes our world. The three sectors that define the public arena are government, the market and community. They each hold varying amounts of power and, accordingly, influence each other and broader society. Illustration 1, below, shows the balance of our current public arena and broader society in various ways.

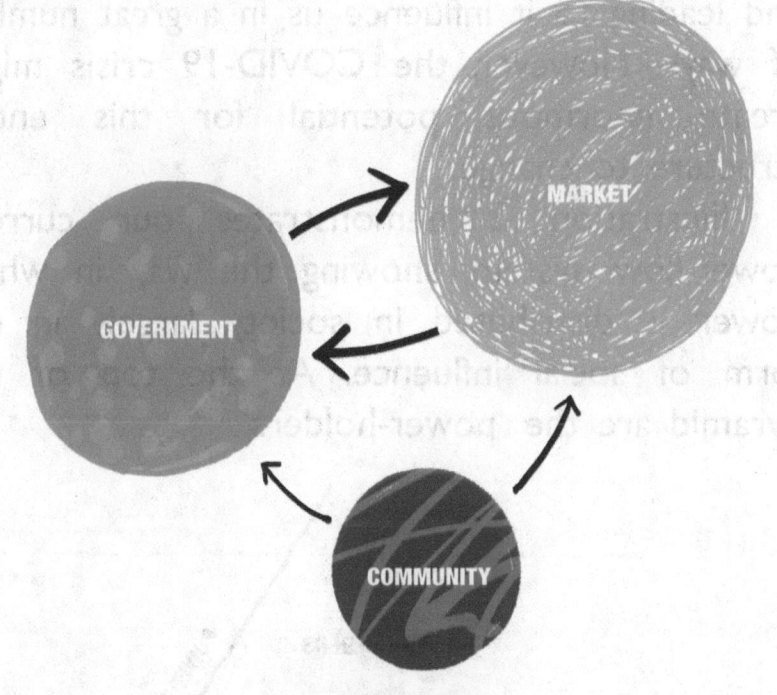

Illustration 1

As you can see, the market holds the bulk of the power, the government has a decent-sized amount, and the community holds very little. Additionally, the market and government are constantly feeding off and influencing each other, whereas the community has a much smaller and less influential relationship with both. This situation means that the community holds little power in our public arena, despite being the most impacted. Most importantly, this simply isn't an equitable situation. Power hasn't been distributed in a way that allows for accountability, giving the market total dominance over society and leading to it influence us in a great number of ways. However, the COVID-19 crisis might create enormous potential for this entire structure to change.

Illustration 2 demonstrates our current power-flow system, showing the way in which power is distributed in society, largely in the form of social influence. At the top of the pyramid are the 'power-holders'.

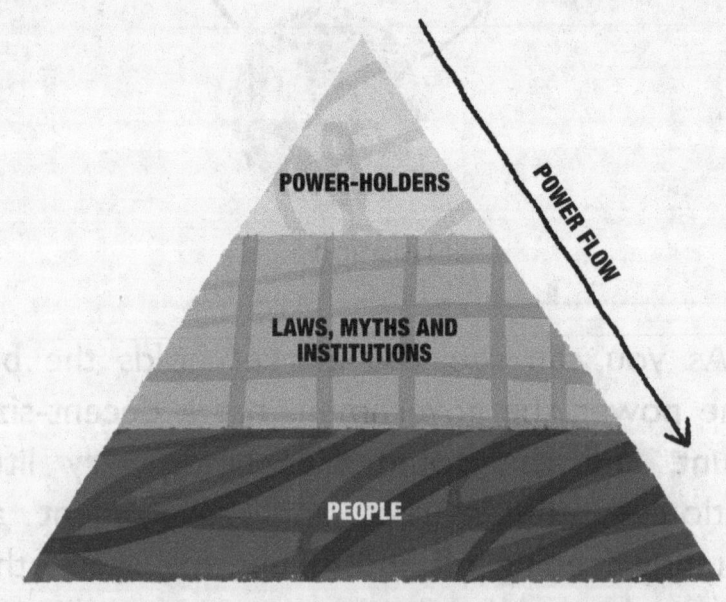

Illustration 2

This might vary from situation to situation, but generally these take the form of government officials and the enormously wealthy. Power and influence begin at this level. Below are laws, myths and institutions. At the bottom of the pyramid are the people. In this system, besides elections and traditional methods of lobbying, there are very few ways for people to influence society as a whole.

What the public arena could look like

Illustration 3 shows what our public arena could look like in an ideal world. Each sector of society would hold equal influence, allowing for a far more democratic and fair society, in contrast with our current system, which is unfairly skewed towards the market. If each sector was of equal power, each would be able to hold the others accountable. This system values all sectors equally, with each providing influence over the others to further positive progress. Realistically, this could take shape in a variety of forms; however, central to levelling this playing field is strong and strategic community organising. By building strong and organised social movements, we can distribute much more power to the community, ensuring that what the people demand can truly influence those other areas. Additionally, the cultures and narratives engulfing the public arena will shift and adjust, creating a more egalitarian and healthy society.

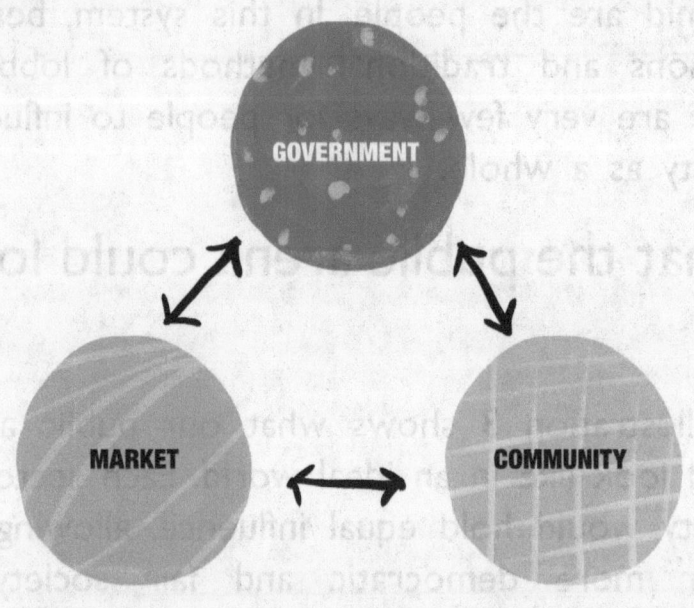

Illustration 3

> **IF EVERY PERSON WHO CARED DEEPLY ABOUT POLITICS AND WANTED TO SEE REAL CHANGE TOOK THE OPPORTUNITY TO SUPPORT CAMPAIGNS AND GROUPS THEY BELIEVED IN, THE WORLD WOULD LOOK LIKE A VASTLY DIFFERENT PLACE.**

Illustration 4 is the 'upside down' power-flow pyramid – radically different to our current system shown in illustration 2. It's a representation of an ideal situation in which the people hold the greatest power and influence, and the current power-holders are placed towards the bottom of the pyramid. In this system, the people would carry far more influence in the shaping of society, providing power far outside the rare official political situation. This system is rooted in non-violent social movements, with support and growth coming from great numbers of people. In both of these visuals, what is always most integral is increasing the power of the community, to make society a much fairer place.

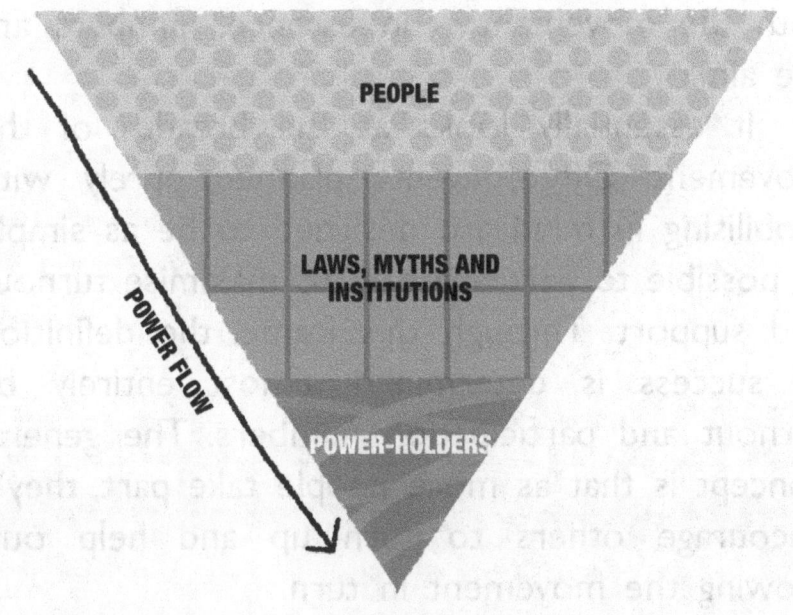

Illustration 4

Mobilising and organising

Something that took me a long time to grasp, and is still one of the central discourses in the activist community, is the notion of *mobilising* as opposed to *organising*. They seem to be very similar concepts, but it's important to understand the difference between the two. Making use of elements from both will help enormously in your creation of intentional and strategic groups.

Mobilising is the sort of activism to which most people are initially inclined. This is about getting as many people as possible to participate in actions and become members or get involved with the movement — in essence, numbers are the aim.

It essentially looks at the breadth of the movement. Often, events planned purely with mobilising in mind are designed to be as simple as possible to participate in, to maximise turnout and support. Through this frame, the definition of success is determined almost entirely by turnout and participation numbers. The general concept is that as more people take part, they'll encourage others to turn up and help out, growing the movement in turn.

These large-scale forms of mobilisation can make for an enormously effective statement, translating into broad events that often garner tens of thousands of people.

Typically, the leadership structures within a group concerned only with mobilisation are quite centralised, and involve people being told an action to take and then encouraging others to do so. Mobilising might look like a giant rally or a massive network of action groups. However, mobilising alone has its flaws. If not paired with methods of organising, it can get stuck, unable to create a long-lasting and effective movement, causing loss of steam.

Organising is a form of building power through depth, rather than breadth. It's based on a more holistic approach, instead of simply using turnout and numbers as a measure of success. Organisers work both to bring new people into the movement and provide them with training and resources to take on a leadership role. Typically these networks are far less centralised, and rely instead on building relationships and group autonomy to make change. Responsibilities are distributed through networks, ensuring that a diverse range of people can step up and take part in leading. By placing such an emphasis on lifting up future leaders and providing them with this education, these movements tend to have a much longer lifespan. Even after initial goals are met, a strong network of leaders can continue directing the movement. Organising places great value on coalition building and forming meaningful relationships between groups, movements and fellow organisers. By building coalitions of groups and activists, a strong sense of unity and movement solidarity is formed. These allies are able to amplify others' work and voices while finding ways of working together towards a shared goal. This collaboration is integral to the growth of all.

> **ULTIMATELY, BOTH MOBILISING AND ORGANISING ARE NECESSARY TO BUILD STRONG AND SUSTAINABLE MOVEMENTS, WITH NEITHER BEING ENOUGH ON THEIR OWN.**

Large mobilisations of people without a long-term strategy typically end up fizzling out; however, without mobilisation it's difficult for organised groups to exercise their power or encourage people to action in the first place.

CHAPTER 3
TAKING YOUR FIRST STEPS

Choose your issue

What's the issue *you* care most about? What do *you* think urgently needs to change?

It might seem remarkably obvious, but the very first step in any form of activism is figuring out exactly what issue you want to take action on. It's likely you already know what this is, or at least have a rough idea of it; however, it can sometimes be difficult to pinpoint one particular sector into which to put most of your effort. You'll come to find that most activists work in a whole variety of areas – you certainly don't need to restrict yourself to just one. However, finding a particular place to focus your efforts on can help you be as powerful as possible, and provide a launch pad to becoming more involved within activism. If you're anything like me, you might be passionate about a broad variety of topics, from mental health and LGBTQ+ rights, to Indigenous land sovereignty and the treatment of refugees, so narrowing it down can be a struggle. (It's also important to note how these issues intersect in a variety of ways; in order to have true social justice you mustn't leave anyone behind.)

Take some time to look at the issues you *really* care about. Is there anything in particular that jumps out at you for some reason?

Maybe you see one issue as the most urgent of all, or another as completely ignored and under-represented? Is there something you feel a particular personal connection with? Or have you noticed a topic that has nowhere near enough manpower in the movement behind it?

If you still feel that you want to be involved all over the place, then it's worthwhile exploring a variety of these passions. You don't need to consume yourself with each and every one, but if you put some work into researching further, volunteering a little time with action groups and learning about different movements, you'll discover the places you enjoy the most and where you feel you're the greatest asset. As time progresses, you might notice you're drawn to one issue more than another, and this focus might shift again later, and that's okay! This is a lifelong journey of self-discovery and education; it is in no way a static mould you have to squeeze yourself into.

Despite being relatively new to activism, I have already been involved in a large number of issues. Although the amount of my personal activity has varied, I've directly worked with groups specialising in marriage equality, changing the dialogue around sexual assault, bringing awareness to menstrual inequity, and fighting the climate crisis. And that isn't even including the many rallies and protests I've attended, and the groups I support in different ways. However, I have certainly found my home in the climate space.

Since first learning about the sheer severity of the climate crisis, and the ways in which politicians have been able to sweep concerns under the carpet, I've felt an enormous drive to make change in some sort of way. I think what has made it most energising and confronting to me is the scale of the crisis itself, and the ways in which it impacts far beyond the surface level.

As a young person, it's near impossible not to grow angry and feel a sense of desperation at the lack of input I have around decisions that will greatly (and usually negatively) influence my life.

And, while it's terrifying to imagine how my future will look, it's far scarier to consider the futures of those in less privileged positions. People are *already* dying in enormous numbers due to the climate crisis: ecosystems are collapsing, oceans are rising, species are depleting, natural disasters are more frequent and intense, and food insecurity is growing greatly. In essence, our entire planet is off kilter. The people who are feeling these impacts first and the worst are almost always the least privileged – Black and Indigenous people of colour, developing nations, refugees, remote communities, people of lower economic status, and so on. Knowing that this situation exists, I couldn't help but panic. I had an overwhelming and crushing realisation of just how small I was, and just how little influence I had. I remember passively watching the Al Gore climate documentary, *An Inconvenient Sequel*, which followed the development of the Paris Agreement in 2015–16, and not being able to hold back tears. We were – and still are – facing impending disaster, yet seemingly no one was willing to do what it takes to change things. I felt so isolated and, if I thought too hard about it, as if I was going to be sick.

If I'd followed that feeling, and shut myself off from what was important, I wouldn't have allowed myself to make a change. I would have continued feeling powerless and small and let myself stay like that.

But, along the way, I realised I could not in good faith continue going about my day-to-day life without doing everything I could to alleviate the crisis.

It's also important to establish why you feel so passionate about an issue, and what led you to this point. This might be something gargantuan, or perhaps a tiny impact that continues to motivate you. Take some time to explore the problem: are you personally impacted by it, or do you have family or friends who are? Did your parents raise you according to these values, or did you stumble across them yourself? Why does this issue resonate with you more than other issues? Think of this as the *who, what, when, where, why, how* of your ideologies. It's okay if the answers don't come to you right away; typically, what leads us to believe in something is a massive amalgamation of various experiences and moments that build to a particular opinion.

Get educated

So, you've figured out what area(s) you want to get involved with. Amazing! The next step is simply putting in the time to thoroughly educate yourself on whatever cause you're wanting to support. I'm not saying that you need to suddenly transform into a fully qualified expert on the topic (although it wouldn't hurt!), but that you should feel confident in what you know and comfortable in expressing the information. This is necessary for informing the choices you make as you develop your strategy and messaging, but also ensures you're committing to something you're properly informed about and truly know is the right thing.

At this point, Google actually *is* your best friend. Take time to read through webpages, articles and op-eds that show a variety of different perspectives, to start to see a fuller picture. Take note of the general information and the most interesting and useful statistics you find – having these for future reference can be super helpful. A large part of this research stage is ensuring that you are consuming high-quality information with a scientific backing, rather than blindly trusting everything you read and see. The best way to do this is to check the source of all the information you find: scientific pieces should ideally be peer reviewed and recently conducted, and the larger the sample size the better. It's also important to consume information from those most directly impacted; first-person experiences are equally as valuable as quantitative research. And Google most certainly isn't the end of your research. There are many documentaries, podcasts, books, essays, films and TV shows that provide information in a digestible and engaging way.

As you learn, take time to challenge your beliefs and question why you think the way you do. Don't be afraid to ask questions: nobody is born with all the answers.

Once you've established this groundwork of knowledge, your work is nowhere near over. What is most vital for an effective activist is the ability to learn, develop and ultimately grow into a better and more understanding change-maker.

> **AT NO POINT WILL YOU HAVE EVER FINISHED LEARNING: THERE IS ALWAYS A PERSPECTIVE YOU HAVEN'T YET HEARD, A LEADER WHOSE ADVICE YOU HAVEN'T YET RECEIVED, AND A LESSON YOU'VE YET TO LEARN.**

What makes the world of activism so powerful, though, is that it's a place of constant education, starting from the bottom up. Every single person wants to lift others up and find ways to share as much information as possible. As long as you are always curious, willing to learn from others and grow as an activist, you'll be okay.

Start volunteering

Now it's time to put all this information into action! The biggest step you can make towards becoming an activist is to get involved with other groups, to start making connections and learning together. There's a plethora of action groups out there, covering nearly every issue imaginable – they are always looking for more people to join and aid them in making change.

Not only do they tackle a huge variety of issues, but every group that's taking action does so in a slightly different way. Part of your journey as an activist will be working with different groups and people until you find the places where you fit best.

Activism exists in many forms, and what you turn out to enjoy the most and be best at might surprise you. While the stereotypical image of a change-maker might be of them holding a megaphone at a protest, this is in no way the limit of what you can do to make a difference. Creating political art, founding a straight–gay alliance at your school, organising unannouced sit-ins at an elected official's office, putting up guerilla art installations, joining a political campaign, creating digital resources, or surveying on behalf of a group are just a fraction of what can fall under the umbrella of 'activism'. The only way to discover what you're most suited to is to spend time trying out whatever you're inclined towards.

The best place to learn is always on the field. By joining pre-existing groups, you'll be able to explore the activist space in your community and gain real-world experience without the pressure and intensity of starting a whole new group from scratch. The initial connections you make are invaluable; it's remarkable how much they can come in handy down the line. Finding these mysterious groups to join is easy – the best place to start is a local action group or a particular campaign that excites you, such as saving an important public space or service. Many broader organisations have localised action groups that seek to make change within a small-scale location, typically a suburb or electorate. Working with these sorts of groups helps give you a detailed understanding of the intricacies of the politics in your community, and teaches you the groundwork for how to take action.

These groups are usually very easy to get involved with. If they are part of a broader movement, you should be able to find their information on their main website. Additionally, action groups generally have a social media presence – most often a Facebook page or Instagram profile – so you can message them to ask if you'd be able to help. The best place to start is to tell them a little about yourself and your level of experience, and that you'd like to be involved. You don't need to say anything special, simply indicate your interest in joining. These groups often have regular meetings, which are a great way to meet local activists and participate in the group. If you choose to go to one of these meetings, try to approach others and connect with the rest of the group. Other activists love to see new people getting involved, and are generally very welcoming and willing to get into conversation. And, while it's always helpful to find youth-led groups, if you're like me and didn't even realise youth-centred action groups existed, then you needn't ever be discouraged by a big group of oldies! They will love you attending meetings more than you could imagine.

Nail your concept

If you're aiming to create your own group or movement, make sure you have a reason to exist on your own. If your goal, methodology and organisational tactics are exactly the same as those of another group, what is the distinction between you? Are you actually helping by being separate, which might entail divisiveness, or might it to be more effective to just join the other group? There are plenty of amazing movements and organisations out there and, while I'm certainly not discouraging you from initiating another, do ensure that there's a notable enough difference between each of you, and that you're helping the broader movement by being in a separate space.

When you're building a movement, it's vital to find a fresh and creative approach, rather than simply repeating what is already being done. There is great value in doing something that feels new and invigorating; however, this doesn't mean you can't take inspiration from what has worked in the past, but do try to find a technique that isn't currently being overdone. Part of the reason the school strikes were so successful is that they took a step (actually 'striking') that hadn't already been done by young people in relation to the climate. We had seen that rallies and petitions and letter writing and every other 'appropriate' way of going about trying to make change was consistently being ignored by adults in leadership positions, and that the voices of young people in particular were discredited due to our lack of official democratic power. Striking was seen as a radical idea; it was how we, as young people, finally stood up and showed just how much we cared about this issue. Doing something totally different, rather than playing by the rules, led to much more attention and interest being directed at us. It felt fresh and exciting and, finally, it was a movement over which young people could feel a sense of ownership.

In part, finding a fresh approach is about looking for a 'gap in the market'. Look at what already exists around you: which groups are having success, what they are demanding, which voices are being amplified, which forms of action are being taken, which people are engaged, and so on. Be inspired by what is working, and take note of what people really care about. Then, look at what's missing – which people don't have a platform, what types of action are lacking, what sort of organising needs more effort, what issues are being ignored, which people aren't engaged, and so on. If there is something people are angry about, but certain voices aren't being uplifted, find ways in which you can highlight and amplify them. If there's an issue that far too few people seem to care about, find ways to educate and change public sentiment. If people are angry about something but there isn't an effective movement helping them to use that energy to make change, create a place to enable that. Find what is missing, and fill that gap.

You could explore issues within your school, suburb or electorate, your city, state, country, or even internationally. You'll tend to find that there are few spaces designed to have young people at the front taking active leadership positions, in particular POC or regional and rural young people. However, it's important to make sure you aren't taking up space which other people need more. If you aren't directly harmed by an issue, or already see yourself represented and given a platform in most spaces surrounding it, then it's quite likely you'll create a more positive impact by providing support to pre-existing initiatives, which uplift and aid those existing in the margins. There is a major difference between passing the mic to those who need it and speaking on behalf of others, and it's vital not to get the two confused. You'll come to realise that often those described as 'voiceless' are perfectly capable of speaking up, but are so rarely given the opportunity to.

Look at other youth-led movements around the world. There is something special about young people taking charge, and they typically have great success. It's interesting to see how this domino effect of inspiration can happen. For example, in March 2018 the March For Our Lives took place – a series of enormous rallies held throughout the United States in the aftermath of the Marjory Stoneman Douglas High School shooting in Parkland, Florida. Instead of accepting politicians' empty thoughts and prayers and their constant rejection of politicisation of gun-violence deaths, students from the school launched a movement to implement common-sense gun-safety laws. Several months later, Zero Hour held their youth climate march, which attracted a thousand people to the front of the White House in one of many marches held throughout the country. After hearing about both of these, Greta Thunberg initiated her month-long school strike outside the Swedish parliament, demanding climate action in the lead-up to their general election. After reading an article about Greta, Harriet O'Shea Carre and Milou Albrecht from Castlemaine, Victoria, became inspired, as they too felt enormously frustrated about the climate crisis. They grew to launch School Strike 4 Climate, who organised our first Australian strike on 30 November 2018. This garnered massive international media attention, giving the climate strike movement a boost as it began to spread much further globally. Every step of the way, different youth groups were inspiring each other, snowballing into huge movements.

Know who you are

Once you have your cause and you're ready to get to work, you need to define your **theory of change,** your **vision** and your **mission statement** in order to clarify your beliefs and goals as a group. Though these might sound like minor technicalities, each completely shapes your movement. Make sure to spend time brainstorming all three of them.

A **theory of change** is a way of creating a link between the problem and the solution, which forms a basis for strategic planning. Most simply put, it's how you think you can best get from point A to point B. It's a deconstruction of what you think is causing the issue, and what the solution looks like and how you believe it will be best achieved. A theory of change is an important thing to figure out as it informs and impacts all decision-making and campaigning done as a group. It is best kept to one or two sentences, if possible (although some span multiple paragraphs or pages). For example, SS4C's theory of change is: *By building community power and active public support for our solutions, we will compel government and business to serve community interests, not vested interests, in the face of the climate crisis.*

Your **vision** is what you are fighting for the world to look like. As a group, understanding your vision is vital in informing all that you do. This needs to be a clear statement about what you want to see different in the world, although it doesn't necessarily need to cover specific policy or exact changes, unless relevant. You'll find that members of a movement might have slight fluctuations between their visions; however, it's important to find the intersections between them. For example, most people have different images for how they see a sustainable and post-climate-crisis world. Some might think a near totally solar-fuelled future would be best, while others could be more interested in reforestation and wind turbines. While there are discrepancies between the two, they're both fighting for a world in which carbon emissions are greatly lowered and our way of life is as sustainable as possible. Take time to discover your own personal vision and what you want to achieve from activism, and have open dialogues with others you're working with to find an ultimate vision.

Your **mission statement** is how you fall into the broader group making change. This is a statement summarising you as a group, and what you're seeking to be overall. It should outline why you exist, the people you are made up of, who you seek to help, and how you will help the issue. This should be quite short – typically only about a sentence long – and relatively simple. For example, the Australian environmental group, Tipping Point, is to: *Grow the Australian grassroots climate movement by building and supporting grassroots networks to help win campaigns that keep fossil fuels in the ground and accelerate us towards clean energy for all.* And to *Support these networks to take bold, sustained and creative action that shifts decision makers and puts our issues in the spotlight, creating space for change.*

Learn to map power

Power mapping is a very useful tool to identify which allies within your community are most valuable to your cause, and which opposition is best to target. What's so great about it is that it can be done on almost any scale – as small as within your school community, or on a much larger and broader level, such as across your state or country. The system works through identifying the varying levels of influence and support for your group within the community.

To begin, get a piece of paper and draw one line across the middle horizontally and one vertically. Now label the top of the page 'most influence', and the bottom of the page 'least influence'. Do the same on the left and right with the 'most' and 'least supportive', so your page looks like this.

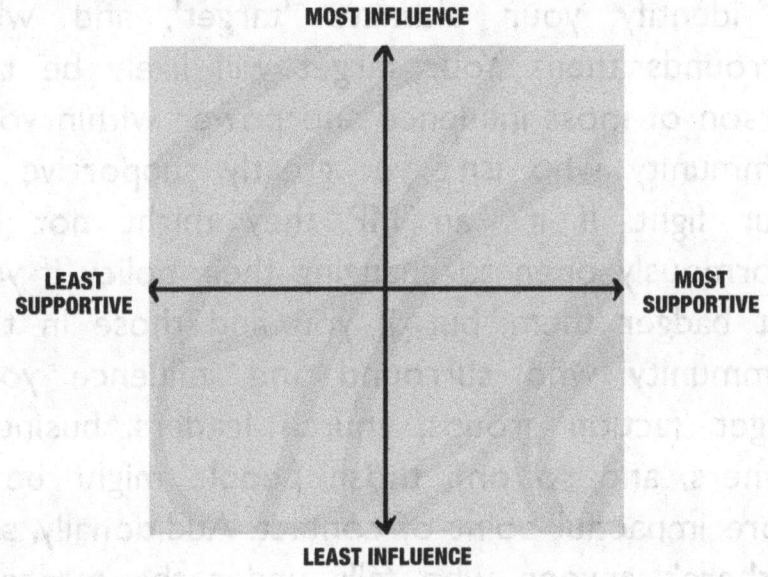

Now it's time to brainstorm! Think about everyone of relevance within your space, then place them on the chart according to their level of broader influence and personal support for your cause. For example, a school principal or local politician is likely to rank quite high on the level of influence, while an action group that hasn't met in six months is likely to be far lower down. Take time to consider individuals and groups on all sides of the issue.

Once you've mapped out every significant figure or group within your community, it's time to start analysing your results. This work is immensely helpful in informing the development of strategy, as those most worthwhile for targeting can often be quite surprising. Take time to identify your ultimate 'target', and who surrounds them. Your target will likely be the person of most influence and power within your community who isn't yet greatly supportive of your fight. If it's an MP, they might not be enormously open to changing their policy if you just badger them; but, if you find those in the community who surround and influence your target, (action groups, church leaders, business owners, and so on), those people might be a more impactful point of contact. Additionally, see if there's anyone who falls under the category of 'influential *and* supportive' who you somehow haven't been in touch with yet. And, if you're already in contact, spend time considering whether you're utilising the connection in the best way possible.

Know your enemy

With any social issue, there are systems, beliefs, incentives, groups and individuals who are allowing the problem to exist in the first place. These might be specific, such as a particular insurance company providing services for a mine, or they could be more general, such as positive public opinion surrounding it. In essence, they are the pillars of support that hold up the problem at hand. Think of this as one of those old Roman buildings – the ones held up by a multitude of columns: the building itself is structurally sound; however, with each column removed it becomes slightly less so. Eventually, when you've destroyed enough of the columns, it can't stand upright anymore and will quickly turn into a pile of rubble. Social issues are just the same. In order to solve a problem, you need to knock down the pillars one by one, dismantling the systems which enable the problem, until there isn't enough support left and it cannot exist. This way of thinking was first developed by Robert L. Helvey in his book *On Strategic Nonviolent Conflict* (2004). While he discusses the pillars in terms of 'oppressive government and foreign occupation', it's a strategy applicable to any structure of injustice, whether broad or more precise.

The #StopAdani campaign is a great example of how organisers were able to identify the major pillars supporting the issue, and systematically work through each one. The Adani mine is a planned Carmichael coal mine in the Galilee Basin in Queensland, first proposed in 2010 by the Indian energy mogul Adani Group. If constructed, it's set to release 4.6 billion tonnes of carbon pollution into our atmosphere, have a disastrous impact on local ecosystems and biodiversity, destroy vast amounts of Indigenous land and water, gain access to 270 billion litres of Queensland's precious groundwater for 60 years for free and only produce, at most, 1500 permanent jobs in the process. Despite initially being planned to be the largest mine of its kind in the Southern Hemisphere, through consistent community-led campaigning it's been forced to downsize from a 16.5-billion-dollar project to only 2 billion self-funded dollars. The very basis of the #StopAdani campaign has been to systematically tear down every pillar of support for the Adani mine.

At the beginning of the campaign, some of the key pillars of the Adani mine included:

Public finance: The Queensland government was considering providing a 1-billion-dollar loan to Adani, and to subsidise the mine by billions.

Private finance: A large number of banks, including the 'big four', were willing to help fund or insure the mine.

Public support: Many saw the mine as beneficial to the local and state economy, and a plethora disagreed with the need to reduce fossil fuels in the wake of the climate crisis.

Approvals: The mine required a variety of environmental approvals in order to be constructed.

Indigenous consent: As the mine was proposed on the land of the Wangan and Jagalingou people, an Indigenous Land Use Agreement was required.

After targeting, here is how those pillars currently stand at the time of writing:

Public finance: The billion-dollar loan was not achieved, and a proposed royalty deal has been delayed multiple times and still not been arranged. However, the mine is still entitled to coal subsidies.

Private finance: 31 financial companies have decided not to help fund the mine, and 68 companies have ruled out involvement with the mine.

Public support: The majority of Australians are against the mine; however, local communities are still largely in support.

Approvals: All necessary approvals have been met; however, the group is facing legal challenges over a water pipeline plan.

Indigenous consent: Indigenous Land Use Agreement has been secured; however, members of the Wangan and Jagalingou clan were excluded, with many still saying no to the mine.

While not every pillar of support has been fully deconstructed or neutralised at the time of writing, Adani still faces economic difficulties and are yet to begin digging for coal, despite pursuing the mine for a decade. This is entirely due to the #StopAdani campaign doing everything in its power to delay and ultimately prevent the mine from being built.

Pillars of support might fall into a range of categories – economic, social, political, and so on. They might be very small – even seemingly insignificant – or broad and intimidating. Take time to really consider the issue at hand and slowly uncover its pillars of support, through thorough research and examination of the problem from as many perspectives as possible.

Techniques such as power mapping are very helpful in identifying some initial pillars. Once you understand the structures supporting your issue, you can be far more strategic and effective in your activism.

Public messaging – be clear about your demands

As a movement, you will be constantly reminding the public about your issue, whether that is before, during or after any sort of lobbying or direct action. There's a lot of competition for people's attention, so you will need to frame your issue in such a way that it sticks in people's minds. As a group, you must determine what your public messaging will look like and how you'll present yourselves. Your message needs to be easy to understand and easy to remember. Your supporters should feel confident in knowing exactly what they're fighting for.

Having a short and clear set of demands is crucial. Three to five main demands is generally a good amount: the more concise the better. For example, UK Student Climate Network have these four demands:

- **SAVE THE FUTURE** – The Government should declare a climate emergency and implement a Green New Deal to achieve Climate Justice.
- **TEACH THE FUTURE** – The education system should be reformed to teach young people about the urgency, severity and scientific basis of the climate crisis.
- **TELL THE FUTURE** – The Government needs to communicate to the general public the severity of the ecological crisis and the necessity to act now.
- **EMPOWER THE FUTURE** – For as long as UK democracy is conducted through a

representative system, everyone over the age of 16 living in the UK must have the right to vote in elections that are conducted via proportional representation, so that everyone's vote is worth the same and this is reflected in our government.

School Strike 4 Climate has these three demands:
- No new fossil-fuel projects, including the Adani mine.
- Full renewable energy and exports by 2030.
- A just transition and job creation for those employed in the fossil-fuel sector.

You will notice that most of these demands don't outline a step-by-step plan on how the goals might be achieved; however, they're specific enough that the goals are very clear. While you should, of course, be able to prove that each of your demands is realistic, it is the role of policy-makers to configure the ins and outs of how they might be implemented, particularly as there will be many different ways to approach them.

When determining your demands, start by looking at what similar groups are trying to achieve. Note if there are overall demands, exact policies or consistent deadlines that pop up, and explore why that might be. By doing this, you should be able to determine which demands and timeframes are necessary and achievable.

If you're working on a smaller scale – within your electorate or suburb, for example – your demands will usually be precise and specific. But, as you continue to work and build to a larger scale, often your demands will become broader and less specific, as they cover a wider area. Be sure to review and revise your demands regularly, although it would be uncommmon to make large changes to them.

Along with your short list of main demands, you might create a separate document to both expand on these goals and include more specific and extensive demands. This allows you to go into greater depth on how you feel issues should be approached, and cover more ground on particularly complex issues.

Intersectionality

In fighting for any social issue, it's vital to have a core message that values intersectionality.

This means recognising the intersections between social issues, and how those people who are lacking inherent privilege are always the most affected by issues, due to preexisting systems of oppression.

Intersectionality can be a confusing concept to wrap your head around, but it's worthwhile taking time to understand it. Essentially, it means recognising how every social issue overlaps in some way, whether that's climate change and feminism, or racism and transphobia.

It also means understanding that someone who lacks privilege – whether that is because of age, race, gender, sexuality, ability, wealth status and so on – will always be the first and worst impacted by different social issues because of this lack of privilege. A framework of intersectionality should inform all the work you do as a group. If your activism is only fighting in comfortable ways for those already in positions of privilege, then you're not dismantling the issue beyond the most surface level. You should be practising allyship wherever possible, and attempt to modify your processes internally alongside external actions as such. Part of this process is constantly questioning what you do, and how you can improve. This might include questions such as: What is your purpose? Who are you serving? What difference are you making? Which voices are you uplifting? Who makes up your team? Where are you falling short?

This is something you must continuously make a conscious effort to do. When I completed the first draft of this book, I sent out copies to various changemakers and friends, inviting them to take a first look, including the wonderful Carly Findlay, a disabled writer, speaker, and appearance activist. She sent me a lovely response, though also let me know that what I had written lacked a lot of information regarding accessibility.

In complete honesty, I felt somewhat nauseous as I read her email back. My thoughts began to race. How could I have missed something so important? Did Carly hate the book? What if she was mad at me? Though after a minute, I took a breath and calmed myself down. Slipping into a panic and worrying about myself didn't help anyone, and only served to distract from action that needed to be taken. I reminded myself that this is what allyship and growth is about – everyone will fall short at points, though whether you amend your errors and change your behaviour to do better going forwards is entirely up to you.

I educated myself further with the resources Carly sent me, and made sure to incorporate these learnings and her advice into the book. The only way to be an activist who genuinely prioritises intersectionality is through doing your best to listen to and take on what those in different positions of privilege have to say. Don't take it personally; if someone takes the time to make you aware of where you can do better, the best response will always be an open mind and a willingness to change.

The following is an interview with Carly Findlay.

How did you first become involved in activism, and what work do you currently do?

I started writing professionally online in 2010 – I was writing on my blog which led to me writing about disability issues for news and government websites. And then I presented on a disability themed community TV. Through writing – and reading work by other disabled people – I learnt a lot about myself. I came to identify as disabled. Through writing, I explored the feeling of what it was like to have a severe skin condition, both medically and the discrimination I endure. And through writing and interviewing people for community TV, I met more disabled people and learnt about many more issues impacting us.

I guess becoming an activist was just accidental – it happened through consistent writing and building an audience.

What does intersectionality mean to you?

Intersectionality means that different identities intersect – race, colour, disability, gender, sexuality, culture, religion, class. A community group is not homogenous. It is not enough to only hear from white, cis-gendered, non disabled people. We must hear from intersectional people, and those with privilege – including me – must pass the mic on.

It's only been in recent years that I've explored my own intersectionality, and identified as a woman of colour. Because of my skin condition, ichthyosis, it is not apparent to those who don't know my family background; and also because living with ichthyosis takes up a lot of emotional energy, especially due to the daily micro-aggressions and overt discrimination faced.

My mum is a Coloured South African (the term she uses) and my Dad is a white Englishman. They courted illegally and in 1981, moved to Australia to get married due to the Apartheid (racial segregation law) in South Africa.

How can people prioritise accessibility in the work they do?

Don't just remember disabled people, disability issues, access and inclusion on International Day of People with Disability (3

December). Make disability a priority all year round. Buy our art, read our stories, listen to our music, create accessibility, call for better media representation, pay us for our lived experience and advice, and give us a seat at every table – every day.

Make access the default, not something that needs chasing up. I really think businesses and individuals need to think less about accessibility and inclusion being a risk, and more about it being an opportunity. Don't be scared. Just start doing it.

I also ask non disabled people to sit with that feeling of discomfort and their non disabled privilege and vow to do better to be a better ally.

Do you have any advice for someone starting out as an activist?

Start small. Small acts can create big change. Amplify voices that are less heard. Hand your platform over to others.

Your activism won't be for everyone – and that's okay. But you will find your people in activism. Make sure you've got lots of support around you. It can be draining and sometimes lonely. Take time to debrief with trusted friends and family, and do something nice for yourself regularly.

> If you've helped just one person through your work, you've done a good job.

Think strategy and tactics

Understanding the difference between strategy and tactics – and then trying to focus conversation on only one or the other – can be a challenge initially. Although they are different on a conceptual level, as soon as you begin discussing one, the other has a tendency to poke its nose in and invade the conversation. But by thinking through both strategy and tactics in an in-depth way, you'll be able to design impactful actions.

Strategy is incredibly important in the world of activism. It's what enables movements to maintain momentum and ultimately succeed in achieving their goals, transforming what might at first glance appear to be a random collection of actions and campaigns into a great force of change.

In the context of organising as a movement, strategy is a plan of how to get from where you are to where you want to be. It's almost like a map, showing the directions of travel and the goals to hit before you make it to your final destination.

Each step of the way is outlined, not by the type of action or techniques to be utilised, but as checkpoints to be achieved along the way. These steps could be vague, such as generally 'raising awareness' about an issue, or very specific, such as 'receiving media attention from every major news company in the country'. Whatever the steps might be, they don't in any way outline *how* you'll achieve these aims. This is about laying the groundwork from where you'll decide which actions you should be taking.

Tactics are the methods you use to bring this strategy to fruition. They can be almost anything – as long as they have the intention and means of attaining the strategy outlined. For example, mainstream media saturation and bringing the climate crisis to the forefront of the public eye are points of strategy; striking during school hours is a tactic to acquire these points of strategy. Ultimately, while strategy shows *what* needs to be achieved, tactics are *how* you will achieve it.

Your strategy is informed by a few main points:
- An analysis of the problem – what is the issue? The answer will probably be 'climate crisis', 'police brutality' or 'menstrual equality'.

- An idea of the broad solution – again, keep this brief. For example, 'transition to renewable energy', 'defunding the police' or 'free access to menstrual products'.
- Your theory of change – as explained on Step 5 in section entitled "Nail your concept".
- How you will bring this theory of change to fruition – utilising your vision and mission statement (from Step 5 in section entitled "Nail your concept"), along with your movement's goals.

I know from experience that when you first start organising it's very easy to come up with heaps of great tactics without fleshing out the strategy behind them. Before you go into planning the specifics of any action, the strategy needs to be developed.

> **WHILE YOU MIGHT HAVE SOME REALLY INTERESTING IDEAS FOR TACTICS, THEY WON'T END UP HAVING A GREAT LONG-TERM IMPACT IF THERE ISN'T A STRATEGY BEHIND THEM.**

The strategy acts as the foundation on which to build your tactics and it's helpful to spend time separately planning both. Before you even consider what your tactics will be, you need to determine an end goal of your action, and what you want the short-term and long-term outcomes to be. Even a really great and interesting tactical idea can't be put to the best use unless it aligns with the strategy proposed.

Once you've figured out your strategy, it's time to use this groundwork to start coming up with ideas for tactics. For me, this is one of the most fun parts of organising; spending time brainstorming all the awesome ways to make change is always an exciting time.

Find like-minded people

Once you've solidified an idea for action, it's time to find a group of like-minded people. This can often be a daunting process, particularly if there is a large amount of disagreement about the issue within your community. However, I can guarantee that you are not alone in caring about this issue and feeling a drive to make change happen; it's only a matter of time before you find the right people to help you out.

What will aid you more than anything in growing your team is a willingness to create genuine connections with others, and seek until you find the people you need. It's definitely tough to set up a group from scratch, but with enough persistence and dedication you'll find your way there.

A good place to start in finding those willing to get on board can be as simple as reaching out to your friends. Chat about your idea with them and see what they think about it, and if it's something they'd want to get involved with. Even if they're not particularly keen, they might know someone else who is.

The internet is also a great place to start making these connections. If you have a social media profile, make a post about your idea and ask if anyone is interested in getting involved in helping you out. You can also reach out for support by posting on relevant public forums, or messaging different activist groups or clubs to see if they could shout you out or provide support.

It's also worthwhile to reach outside your friends and the circles you're already active in. Try school clubs, local activist communities, community groups, and so on – pretty much anywhere you think people might be interested or willing to become active.

When you're approaching people you aren't familiar with, it helps to prepare a brief pitch about your concept and how people can get involved. Then, when you're in a position to talk about it to someone new, you won't get flustered. If the person isn't already aware, explain the issue, and why it's so important to take action. Next, make clear the idea itself and what you are intending to organise. Explain the actual purpose, and what you are trying to achieve by taking action. If they seem interested, discuss how much you'd appreciate them getting involved and how exactly they can do so. Remember, this isn't meant to be formal, simply a way to introduce others to your concept.

For example, if you were launching a campaign to reduce single-use plastics within your community, you might say something along the lines of: 'Right now, we have a major crisis with the continued usage of single-use plastics. As they can't be recycled and take around a thousand years to decompose, when they enter waterways they pose a major threat to marine life. Because they break down into smaller and smaller microplastics, they've entered our food cycle and have even been found in rain. And this is only getting worse. I'm trying to get together a group to launch a campaign for restaurants to stop using plastic straws and cutlery. We'll likely be meeting with restaurant owners to discuss the importance of transitioning away from plastic and helping them to become much more sustainable. We're still in the early stages of pulling a group together, and I was wondering if you'd be interested in getting involved?'

It's also good to get in touch with local allies and find people to support you in different ways. If you've already been involved in local organising, it can be immensely useful to ask for support and mentorship from experienced activists you've worked with previously. However, if you have not yet had contact with a local group, it can be worthwhile sending an email to see if they'd be interested in providing support and help or potentially finding ways to work together. This is all part of building a network of supporters and allies you can rely on for aid and advice.

One of the most integral aspects of succeeding as a movement is encouraging meaningful relationships between the people who are rallying together around the same cause.

> **IT'S NOT AT ALL UNCOMMON FOR RELATIONSHIPS TO BE ENORMOUSLY MISVALUED IN ACTIVISM.**

Often, as we're attempting to make such sweeping changes to the world around us, we feel that relationships are unimportant and come secondary to 'actual activism'. I know this is something I have believed at times, seeing an emphasis on internal relationships as a waste of time and energy that ultimately didn't progress the movement, although they didn't push us backwards either. However, this is an inaccurate and, quite frankly, unhealthy point of view. Relationships between organisers aren't just another pleasant distraction from the real issues, but a necessary step in maintaining the health and effectiveness of a movement.

In joining a movement, we're all coming from a place where we potentially feel quite isolated in the world and the views we hold. It can be tough when you're the only person you're aware of who cares deeply enough about a struggle to be willing to take action. Even if you come from a community of activists, being so aware of the extent of the world's problems can feel draining and difficult to cope with. However, by building these intentional relationships as organisers, we're able to understand each other on a far deeper level. Creating a connection with someone, even if it feels quite surface level, allows for a far greater sense of comfort when working together. If you're in a meeting with a few others you feel comfortable around, it's almost certain that the time you spend together will be far more productive than if you came into the situation with no prior knowledge. Not only does it eliminate awkwardness, but it provides you with the confidence necessary to offer constructive criticism and feedback, which might not have been possible otherwise.

Additionally, these same connections are necessary to ensure tensions and factions don't occur between organisers. When relationships aren't built throughout whole movements, it's very common for minor disagreements to escalate to the point of major tensions, which can cause those of similar ideologies to come together in unofficial factions. When people subconsciously only seek out relationships with those they agree with, it can cause major internal rifts and unfair biases in feedback processes and support. This, in turn, creates tensions, further fuelling the cycle. By having relaxed moments to talk with organisers in the movement, tensions can be avoided and also ironed out if they already exist. This prevents clear-cut factions from being formed, as relationships built throughout the whole group prevent an unintentional groupthink of 'us' and 'them'.

Not only are these connections vital for working together as a team, they're necessary for collaboration and inter-movement connectivity. It's quite common for people to see collaborations as a simple 'transaction' of sorts; however, this misreads the complexity and depth of the process. Collaboration shouldn't mean simply coming to another group with a random idea and seeing if they say yes or no; rather, it should be a long-rooted conversation in which you discover the surprising overlaps in your causes and find ways to work together to achieve a shared goal.

Work as a team

As a movement gains more people, it becomes necessary to develop internal structures and systems to define how it functions. In this process, a mistake that many young organisers make is attempting to build a movement which is far too centralised and hierarchical. Ironically enough, we often imitate the same systems that have led to the very issues we're fighting! This tends to happen due to a variety of factors, including the idea that an 'executive director' and defined national team is somehow more official and diplomatic than the controlled chaos of a non-hierarchical system. Also, as young people, we're frequently told we lack ability and authority, so we tend not to trust other kids taking positions of leadership. However, buying into these ways of thinking only weakens our movements. We need to think carefully through our values as a collective, and let those inform the ways in which we structure ourselves.

The three key things to consider while developing your internal structure are the role of the grassroots, the level of centralisation, and how decisions are made. Ultimately, these won't ever fully determine how power is distributed, as many external factors come into play, but they do play an important part, so it's vital to consider the way in which each one is integrated into your structure.

A **grassroots movement** is one in which members of a community – rather than politicians or big organisations – decide to take action on a local level, which then, through building momentum, naturally spreads to other locations and continues growing. This is a clear bottom-up approach to making change, led by those who truly understand their community and the ways in which they are affected by a particular issue. These campaigns tend to be very impactful, as the power lies with local organisers and relies upon total group autonomy. Demands, strategies and tactics are completely determined by on-the-ground activists, effectively identifying localised problems and finding the best ways to address them. This allows for optimal growth and strength as a group, and ensures that those in need are empowered to take control of their fight.

Without this localised approach, campaigns are forced to take a 'one-size-fits-all' approach to solving problems, which often can't take into account the vast and subtle discrepancies between different contexts. Not only does this prevent power from being distributed within the community that needs it most, but it can also make those in disagreement feel further isolated from the issue. For many, it can be frustrating to have a group or idea being promoted within your community that is visibly coming from outside sources who lack an understanding of your opinion and context. It can feel as if you're being treated as 'yet another place to fix' by those outside your area rather than a unique landscape in which you understand what's best for yourself.

However, with a grassroots approach, everyone within the community has a voice (whether for or against) and, as meaningful dialogue is exchanged, it's more likely to reach unification between sides and the most agreeable solutions. This is a form of flipping the power flow pyramid on its head, placing civilians and those traditionally lacking power in the driving seat of change.

What allows grassroots movements to gain power is deep organising. In order for communities to be uplifted and understand how to go about making change, local leaders need to be grown through education, mentoring and the sharing of resources. For this to happen, we need to develop specific systems of mentoring and education to continue building each other up. This might be through implementing a buddy system between more experienced volunteers and those with less confidence, having monthly education calls, or assigning local leaders to ensure there's a point of contact for any questions.

Decentralisation within an organisation is the process by which power and decision-making abilities are fairly distributed through a network, creating a horizontal system of operating. In complete decentralisation, no person is deemed more 'important' or of higher authority than anyone else, meaning anyone wanting to get involved and take a position of local leadership is able to. Decisions are made hyper-democratically, and anyone can choose to propose an idea for the group. This is extremely important in ensuring the long-term success of a movement. Not only are people constantly upskilling and able to take on however many tasks they'd like according to their personal capacity, but they feel a genuine sense that they're making a difference. The core issue with only allowing a select group of people to lead decision-making or strategy is that it leaves little motivation for those beneath. While they wanted to get involved so that they could make a tangible change to the world, but instead they find themselves placed in a position of simply following instructions and with no sense of autonomy. Not only does this drain motivation for being active, but it also prevents the movement from being as effective as it could be if it were constantly educating and mentoring new people.

Despite this, decentralisation mustn't be confused with structurelessness. A complete lack of any structure will cause movements to fizzle out prematurely, before eventually collapsing. Instead, a variety of internal systems, such as set voting procedures, proposal implementation, working-group creation and so on, are all required to maintain a long-lasting and well-functioning group. For example, SS4C are a completely decentralised and grassroots group, yet have seemingly infinite internal procedures and processes between our dozens of local hubs and national organising space.

However, even in grassroots-led decentralised movements, work needs to be done on a national level and local group interconnectedness remains an important point of developing strategy. To approach this work on a national level, it's helpful to maintain a horizontal power structure, while also allowing for decisions to be made and the movement to progress. One popular method of going about this is a working-groups structure. A working group is a team of people who work together in developing and solving issues in the same area. There is a huge variety of ways to implement this, but they all follow a similar base format: a range of working groups are formed to cover broad internal sections of the movement, such as media, wellbeing, strategy and so on. These working groups are then divided up into more specific working groups based on specialised areas within each broader section. This process continues until further groups aren't needed. Under this type of system, anybody within the movement can join whichever working groups they like, ensuring that as many people as possible are distributed between the different tasks, while also keeping a general sense of cohesion in the group.

Ultimately, finding a structure will take time and experimentation.

THERE'S ALMOST NO CHANCE YOU'LL GET IT RIGHT THE FIRST TIME AROUND – AND THAT'S OKAY.

What's most important is the ability to reflect on what you've created and objectively figure out what is and isn't working, before finding ways to adapt and modify to overcome difficulties. Don't worry about sorting it out right away. Often it's best to work together for a little while and find what feels most natural before making anything official. It can be a long and gruelling process at times, but I assure you it's totally worth it.

Finding an effective method of **decision-making** can again be quite a challenge; every group requires something slightly different. In a group like SS4C, we have a clearly stated method of how decisions should be made, as designed by our structure working group. Anybody can create a local or national proposal outlining any idea they want to implement, created through an 'advice process', involving consultation with various strikers and people outside the movement. On a local level, groups are able to make choices according to whichever system of decision-making they like best. On a national scale, proposals are categorised into 'working group specific' and 'movement-wide' decisions. If the decision will impact only one or two working groups, they are consulted, along with any particular impacted individuals, and asked for their feedback. Any objections and criticisms are taken onboard and the proposal is amended as such until everybody is in support. For movement-wide proposals, a striker will add their proposal to the agenda of a fortnightly national call, and people will leave objections and criticisms before and during the call. These comments are responded to or the proposal is accordingly modified. During the call, a vote is held as to whether the proposal is ready to go ahead to an official national vote. At this stage, at least 67 per cent of people must vote yes for it to go ahead. Then, over the course of the next seven days, the proposal can't be edited at all as the broader movement votes. Again, a 67 per cent majority is required; however, at least 30 votes must be cast for it to be valid. Those proposals that are voted into the network are then implemented over the next few weeks.

Obviously, this system will not work for every movement, particularly those with smaller team sizes, but strategies can be adapted and modified to suit your own needs. Having a typed proposal for every decision is super helpful, so that those who aren't able to make the required calls are as equally well informed when voting. Additionally, having a distinction between large, movement-defining decisions and more specialised ideas helps to ensure national conversation is kept relevant. Requiring a large majority (two-thirds) is in support for any vote to be officialised means approved decisions are always what's best for the movement, and a lengthy advice process makes certain that time isn't wasted on proposals that haven't been well considered.

PART TWO

The activist toolkit

Once you start working together as a team, you want to make sure your efforts count. Not only is activism about putting in the hours to ensure tangible outcomes, but also investing your time and manpower into the places that will most benefit from them. Many of us have worked through these difficulties the hard way, so hopefully you won't be stuck reinventing the wheel. As you and your team learn and develop and eventually nail the techniques, the skills that are involved will begin to feel like second nature. You'll start to find your own ways to make a difference, adding to the vast ecosystem of change-making in the world today. The nitty gritty of it all is effectiveness, and effectiveness comes down to planning.

When I first started organising, I had no clue just how many small details were involved in planning every slightest thing. Nothing can be glossed over, or assumed to 'figure itself out' at some point, or you'll end up with a half-baked form of action. You'll learn to love logistics; for everything to run smoothly everyone must know their role, embrace never-ending checklists, spend far too long in meetings and fully harness the power of the internet. But above all is the need for constant open communication and patience. It's a long and technical process, but the results are well worth it.

CHAPTER 4
LOBBYING POLITICIANS

IN THE WORLD OF POLITICS AND LOBBYING, IT'S INCREDIBLY rare for young people to have any representation. And that – surprise, surprise – is because we can't vote.

There's a common belief held by adults – and by many young people too – that because politicians don't need to worry about preserving our vote, they can ignore us and the issues that matter to us. Unfortunately, this belief is upheld by many in leadership positions, which translates into them making change without considering the benefits or losses to our generation.

> **DESPITE NOT BEING GIVEN AN OFFICIAL SAY, THERE ARE STILL WAYS TO AMPLIFY OUR VOICES AND ENSURE WE CAN'T BE IGNORED.**

Meeting with your local Member of Parliament is an effective way to directly communicate with one of the primary decision-makers in your community. It's a means for you to spark conversation and real-time dialogue about the matters you find most pressing. This can be a daunting part of activism, especially for young people; however, depending on how well prepared you are, and how willing the MP is to genuinely hear you out and consider what you have to say, it can have very real and tangible outcomes.

How not to have a meeting with your MP

An MP is an elected official who represents your area in federal parliament. As part of the 'lower house', they play an important role in passing or rejecting legislation. A Senator is one of multiple representatives of an entire state or territory and makes up the 'upper house'. While MPs serve three-year terms, Senators are elected for a total of six years. If you aren't already aware, figure out who is your local Member of Parliament. You can find them in the Senators and Members list on the Australian Parliament House website (aph.gov.au). If you're looking for your state member, you can find the information on your State Parliament House website.

The first time I had a meeting with an MP, it's safe to say it went horribly. As in, I-cringed-for-most-of-it-and-immediately-regretted-everything-

I-said horribly. Not only had I neglected to prepare for anything except the most surface-level questions, but I also showed up late (and uncomfortably damp from the sprinkling rain). At the time, heaps of School Strike 4 Climate organisers and participants had been working nationally to arrange and attend as many meetings with federal MPs as possible. We had three primary goals we wanted the politicians to commit to: stopping the Adani mine, transitioning Australia to 100 per cent renewable energy, and preventing any new sources of fossil fuels (in particular, coal). I was feeling a little nervous about the meeting, but generally chill – if I'd already done a live TV interview, how hard could a conversation with a single MP be?

Even getting to the office was a challenge. I'd planned my route the day before – already an unusual organisational win on my part! However, I hadn't anticipated a very late bus, which really threw a spanner in my travel plans. I sat at that bus stop for what seemed like an eternity, growing more panicked by the second as I realised how late I was getting. By this stage, I was scrolling compulsively through Google Maps to calculate the pace I'd need to sprint at to plausibly make it there on time – although something told me that turning up out of breath and covered in sweat might look even worse than calmly and coolly strutting in a little late. Finally – 15 minutes late, to be precise – the bus rocked up. It was around this time that I noticed my phone was on 5 per cent charge, and I'd somehow need to ration it for long enough to make it home that evening. As I leapt off the bus near to where the office was meant to be, I was surprised to find that I just couldn't see it. I raced up and down the street a few times before noticing that I had hurried blindly past the building two or three times without realising.

I made my way down a little corridor, where I was relieved to find my fellow striker, Daisy, on a seat in the tiny waiting area. There was also a mother and her two primary-school-aged children, who we had arranged to come to the meeting with us as they had attended the first climate strike. We chatted briefly before the MP came out and greeted us and showed us into the office for our discussion. The two girls both had hand-written letters, with drawings of polar bears, that explained how we needed to stop global warming.

Now, while I think it was great that these younger people came along and were able to experience the opportunity, it did make us appear somewhat less serious when we were there to meet about jobs, renewables and fossil fuels.

However, after 10 minutes or so they left and Daisy and I continued the conversation. We began by asking about our three goals, and what the likelihood would be of the MP's party adopting them. But we were quickly brushed off. Every time we brought up a point, the MP would come up with another excuse or simply say that our data wasn't accurate.

It was around this time that I realised we had made two major errors. Firstly, we hadn't prepared our sources beforehand. If we'd come with very specific statistics to back up our arguments, it would've been impossible for them to brush us off, as they'd managed to do so far, and our case would've sounded significantly more solid. Because we hadn't done this, every time one of our points was rejected we had no evidence to come back with, meaning we grew increasingly flustered and sounded as if we really didn't know what we were doing. Secondly, even if we didn't have those sources when we entered the room, we would've been able to bring them up almost instantly online, but both of us had nearly dead phones and there was no wi-fi we could connect to on our laptops. This process of us our arguments being dismissed and ignored or, even worse, laughed off, carried on for the remainder of the meeting, even as we left the building.

Near the end of the meeting, I used half my remaining phone battery to show the MP just one source — a peer-reviewed report by the Australian National University, outlining exactly how Australia could convert to full renewable energy by 2030. This was met with a laugh and the words: 'Well, [their] scientists didn't agree.' Not only did I feel frustrated with myself at my lack of preparedness, but I was really upset that the MP wasn't willing to treat us like adults and engage in a dialogue with us. It was patronising and condescending and a very humiliating experience; however, I learnt a huge amount from it.

How to have a meeting with your MP

So, as described, meeting with your local Member can be a challenge. Given that they have busy schedules to begin with, and tend to avoid meetings with people who don't like the poor choices they have made, it can feel like an uphill battle to even get an appointment. However, throughout the process, remember that *you* are part of *their* electorate, so they have an obligation to listen to you and the views of the community. They are public servants at the end of the day:

it's their job to represent the area in which you live and make change for the better.

To open communications, send an email to their office requesting a meeting (the office contact information can be found on the Member's website). This doesn't need to be a long email: just say who you are, what group or issue you represent, and then briefly explain the purpose of the meeting, what you would like to discuss and who will be in attendance. If there's anything else that might make you stand out (such as being the leader of or spokesperson for a local group), make sure you include it in the email to improve your chances. Your email might read something like this:

> Hello,
>
> I'm Carole Baskin, and I'm the founder and official spokesperson of Big Cat Rescue. I am based in the electorate of Grayndler, and would like to schedule a meeting with A. Albanese in regards to the bill 'Save Big Cats'. I would like to discuss his views on the captivity of big cats, and explore what he can do to ensure they are kept safely away from private owners. My friend, Michael Smith, will also be in attendance.
>
> I look forward to hearing back from you,
>
> Carole Baskin

While ensuring that your email is concise, try to be persuasive and convey the importance of your meeting. To further register your interest, give their office a call to confirm that they received your email and to state again that you look forward to hearing back from them.

It's fairly common for these requests to go unanswered, so, if you still haven't received a response after about 10 days, give the office another call and request to speak to the MP's personal assistant or diary manager in order to secure the meeting. Try to keep a log of each time you attempt to make contact. If they repeatedly will not confirm anything with you, it's helpful to refer back to these unsuccessful attempts when speaking to office staff. If your request is initially denied, don't lose hope: it isn't uncommon to secure a meeting with an MP purely through persistence.

Remember, throughout the entire process, try to remain calm and polite. To secure a meeting, you need staff to remain inclined to schedule one for you. At the end of the day, everyone you're in touch with during this process is a human being, so treat them with respect and make the experience as constructive as possible.

Once you've been able to secure a meeting, it's time to start preparing for it. It's helpful to have a team of three to four people present at the meeting (make sure the MP's office is aware of this beforehand). With a group of this size, you'll be able to work together in a collaborative way to utilise your strengths without it being too large a crowd, while also projecting a message from a variety of viewpoints and perspectives.

Look into where the MP stands on your issue—
- What have they said about it in the past?
- Is this any different to what they've been saying recently?
- Are they supportive?
- Is it something they've ever addressed before?
- Do others in their party have strong views on the issue?
- Look through public statements they have made, and also how they've voted on similar issues.

I recommend the website theyvoteforyou.org.au to help you find this information, in addition to the politician's own website. Depending on the answers to these questions, you'll have to approach your preparation in a few different ways. Think about what you want to say to the MP, and what you want to achieve from the meeting. It's often helpful to have a few specific outcomes you'd like to achieve. These might be the MP pledging their support for the cause, choosing to vote against a bill, participating in a town hall event, or attending a rally.

Inform yourself on everything you think could be relevant for the meeting. Again, you don't need to be a professional, but you should feel confident in being able to argue your point, particularly against tricky arguments.

If you're the sort of person who doesn't have a great memory, you might want to physically print out some key facts and their sources, which you can refer to during the meeting – but make sure this is simply a reference, rather than a script to read from. Once you feel confident, attempt some practice meetings with group members or friends. When tricky questions come up that you don't know how to answer, make a note and spend some time practising your responses before returning to it at a later point. Ultimately, you want to feel thoroughly prepared and relaxed going into this.

In addition to knowing your facts, it can help if you bring a unique narrative into the room. Statistics and information are important, but relating to someone emotionally can make an argument significantly stronger. Think about the

issue at hand and consider how it impacts you and your community–
- Are you personally impacted in some way?
- Do you have friends or family who are?
- Is there a symptom of the problem that impacts your community in a unique, unexpected, or underrepresented way?

No matter what the issue, with enough thought and conversation a compelling story will arise. Once you've found this story, think about how you want to express it. What particular elements are most important and best demonstrate the point you're arguing? Think about how you can emphasise these, and again draw it back to the central issue. Practise how you will communicate this: it doesn't need to be perfectly rehearsed, but the more comfortable you are with what you're saying, the better.

Once you've figured out what needs to be communicated, make a plan with your group members as to how the meeting will run. Figure out who'll be discussing each point, and what exactly they'll be communicating. This doesn't have to be complicated and rigid; however, it should be detailed enough that everyone feels they're on the same page and is comfortable in knowing how the meeting will run. At this stage, it can be helpful to create a document to physically give to your MP, outlining your key concerns and points, and including some pertinent facts. If you choose to create this document, make sure to print out a couple of spares in case advisors are present during the meeting.

Now it's time to actually have the meeting! While appearances shouldn't be important, in this situation they *do* matter, and can really have an impact on first impressions. You don't need to dress in anything fancy, but make sure you look presentable and well groomed. Ensure you get to the MP's office *at least* 15 minutes early, so that you can run through your notes with your group and ensure everything runs smoothly. The meeting itself can feel daunting, so this extra time allows you a moment to take a breath and chill a little bit. Soon enough, you'll be introduced to the MP. As you meet them, try to maintain eye contact, clearly introduce yourself and your group, and thank them for taking the time to meet you.

When you begin the conversation, take into account their awareness of your issue. If it's a topic they don't know much about, explain the context of the situation and the importance of it. However, if you know they're already aware, you can skip this background information. As you go through your talking points, bear in mind that you're speaking to a real person: while you shouldn't be overtly colloquial and informal, you also don't need to sound as if you're giving a speech to a class at school. And remember, being polite and respectful doesn't mean that you can't take a firm stance. If the MP attempts to refute the information you're providing, explain that it's factual and give the source from which it's derived. If you feel that they aren't responding well to a particular argument or are attempting to brush you off, try switching to another talking point and continue.

Make it clear exactly what you're asking of them. Using your predetermined goal/s, discuss with them the potential of their taking action, and attempt to secure a commitment from them. As you do this, explain the benefits to them.

The number one approach for this is demonstrating the support for the issue from the voters within their electorate.

There's nothing more likely to make an MP shift on an issue than showing that it's an important problem for their constituents.

Look at local polling, refer to petitions, or provide evidence that people likely to vote for them would be in support of what you are suggesting. However, if you're lacking support in your area, you will need to rely more on explaining the *negative* consequences within the electorate if they don't take action. You might want to consider some other incentives you could offer them, such as local media coverage, or a short speaking spot at a rally.

At the end of the meeting, thank the MP and any staff for taking the time to meet with you and state that you'd like to meet again at some point in the future. If there were any advisors present during the meeting, make sure to ask for their business cards. You might want to take a photo with the MP to share later on social media; however, this isn't necessary if you feel that it wasn't a particularly helpful meeting, or that the MP seemed unwilling to take on your goals.

After the meeting, it's time to debrief. As a team, discuss what went well and what could have gone better. Reflect on what the MP was willing to do, and what they seemed against. Make notes on anything that stuck out to you, and what you might change next time you're able to have a meeting with the politician. It's helpful for a couple of people from your group to take on the task of following up with the MP, to ensure that any commitments made are followed through on.

Writing to your MP or Senator

While in-person meetings are ideal, other forms of contact can also have an impact. Writing a letter to an MP or Senator is a great way to make your voice heard, both locally and by those in other locations who you feel are valuable and important enough to make contact with, such as the relevant Minister.

Emailing is certainly an option, but sending a physical letter to a politician is usually the best way to get a response. Similarly, while some online templates for letters read very well, you're far less likely to enter meaningful engagement if you send a carbon copy of the same letter everyone else has sent.

In accordance with the seemingly-necessary-but-somewhat-shallow 'officialness' of everything to do with politicians, letters should be formatted in the correct style.

In the top left-hand corner, write the name and address of the politician.

For a Member of Parliament, this should be written as

<Mr/Mrs/Ms/Dr> <First Name> <Last Name> <MP>.

For a Senator it should be

<Senator> <First Name> <Last Name>.

However, if the politician is a Minister, you add 'the Honorable' to their title; so, for an MP, this would be

< The Hon. > <First Name> <Last Name> <MP>.

For a Senator who is a Minister, it would be

<Senator the Hon. > <First Name> <Last Name>.

Additionally, you then start your letter with even more unnecessarily fancy titles: 'Dear Sir/Madam' or 'Dear <Mr/Mrs/Ms/Dr> <Last Name>' for MPs, and 'Dear Senator' or 'Dear Senator <Last Name>' for Senators.

To begin your letter, explain who you are and the reason you're writing. If you're a member of their electorate, now is the point to make that clear, along with any particular connection you have with the community.

Next, explain your issue and why you're so passionate about it – always try to keep each letter to just one key point. It can be helpful to reference any relevant statistics, explain how you or someone you know has been impacted by the problem, how it specifically relates to your community, and draw on any recent news articles about it. Don't stretch out your point to be unnecessarily long: it should be kept to just one or two pages.

Outline exactly what you want the politician to do in response to the issue – that might be to bring it up for discussion in a party meeting, to attend a local town hall event, to vote a particular way on a bill, or something else. Remember to keep the tone of the letter polite to increase your chance of receiving a response. And you'll need to provide your contact information so they can get back to you: either in the top right-hand corner of a physical letter, or as part of your email signature.

If you've waited for over a month and haven't received a reply, call the office and ask if they've received your letter, and when they expect to get back to you. If you still don't get a response, keep calling every couple of weeks until you do.

When to move on

There reaches a point when lobbying politicians can only do so much. You might try your hardest to communicate honestly and provide a genuine argument for them to respond to, but it's far too common for politicians to brush you off and refuse to take you seriously. Much of the time it can feel, even in the depth of conversation, as if they're robots, approaching every situation knowing all their responses before you've even asked a question, and they will continue dodging your point until they don't have to answer you anymore. And that's when you're lucky enough to have got a meeting; I personally know many campaigners who've been attempting to meet their MP for years and still haven't got a foot in the door. The intensity of this experience is even worse for young people. Despite living in a politician's electorate, simply because we're not quite yet of voting age, our views and opinions are far too often regarded as irrelevant. We're stereotyped as 'self-obsessed and apathetic'; yet, if we proceed to genuinely care about the political decisions impacting our lives, we're labelled 'bratty and brainwashed'. In essence, we can't win.

As long as politicians don't feel under threat of losing their seat, they will continue to ignore those they're supposedly working for, taking us back to the cultural issues with our public arena we discussed in Chapter 2. While the political-lobbying style of activity should certainly hold a place of high importance, it's nowhere near effective enough to really change the world. At that point, tactics need to escalate in order to force politicians to make change happen.

CHAPTER 5

THE ULTIMATE GUIDE TO HOLDING A PROTEST

THE PHYSICAL PUBLIC PROTEST IS ONE OF THE MOST ICONIC methods of activism there is, being the type of event that not only achieves political action, but also brings together everybody who feels passionate about the cause. It's a communal event: as long as you're in that crowd, you know you're among family.

A public gathering is a way to demonstrate both how angry people are, and their willingness to take time out of their day to prove it.

For young people, it is often assumed that we are simply enthusiastic and interested in a topic, as though it is another 'hobby' of ours. Similarly, it's implied that anger, fear and anxiety are inappropriate emotions to motivate behaviour. But these feelings are not only completely valid, but also exactly what we *should* be feeling when an important issue is continuously mismanaged.

> **PROTESTS, AND THEIR ATTENDEES, ARE DRIVEN BY ANGER AND OVERWHELM – AND THERE'S ABSOLUTELY NOTHING WRONG WITH THAT.**

Direct action creates a space for people to direct these emotions in positive ways, finding methods to help make a tangible difference.

If you're hoping to organise a public protest, there must already be a sense of public interest around the issue. Even if there isn't a terribly strong movement to change things, for a protest to be successful, people need to *care* about the problem that is being faced. For this reason, public rallies aren't always the best approach to making change – sometimes campaigning, and focusing on education and awareness, needs to drive public opinion in the right direction first.

However, when the time is right, protests can pack a major punch. This time might be just after a significant moment or event that likely is to – or already has – worsened the issue, or highlighted the importance of action against it. This might be the run-up to a bill being discussed by government, a leader saying something insensitive, a tragedy caused by inaction and so on. If you know that a large proportion of the public is now aware of the issue and sides with you, then a protest is a super powerful way to visibly demonstrate how many people care and are willing to fight for what they see is right. It shows that people don't just have an opinion about the topic, but that they also feel a drive and desire to take to the streets to prove how much it matters to them.

A public protest is also a great way for people to start to get involved in campaigning. Think back to the first time you attended a rally or protest, or, if you haven't yet attended one, look at images and footage online. The passion, excitement and anger is almost tangible in the air around you, like an electric charge. It's a magical thing to experience; despite the overwhelming issues you might be fighting against, you truly know — at least in that moment — that the people can win. If we take hold of this passion and momentum, and create pathways for people to become more involved, it helps to further grow the movement.

After a heap of experience of organising protests, I've collated all my knowledge into the following, very practical guide. You don't need to do these steps in order, and you won't need to do all of them for every protest, but you'll find almost every action will use a combination of the skills explored here.

Step 1: What sort of protest?

We can protest in many ways. There's a plethora of action styles that all help to achieve different goals and outcomes. It's also common to use multiple forms of protest at one event, either combined or one after the other.

While a massive public rally is the classic image of a successful event, you don't need to have an enormous turnout of people for a protest to be effective. With even a small group, you can create an impactful and compelling image that is just as powerful as a giant protest.

Think about Extinction Rebellion, for example, an environmental group that was first initiated in the UK and has since grown into a global movement. They focus on creative (and often illegal) actions to portray the need for climate action in ways we don't usually see – and that have led to thousands of arrests. They often use costume, music, art or movement, and their actions can be dramatic (such as their Red Rebels, who, with painted white faces and in red cloaks and headdresses, walk together slowly in lines, on their own or at bigger events), or occasionally funny (to highlight insect population decline they have held 'die-ins' of people dressed as bees in public areas). These actions often only involve a small group, yet still portray a powerful message.

Just a few styles of protest include:

Rally: One of the most common forms of protest, a rally is a mass gathering of people to fight for a particular cause. Speakers and performers will typically present throughout the event.

March: A march will often go hand in hand with a rally or other large mobilisation. This entails the group travelling together to a set location.

Sit-in: This method of occupation protest involves a group peacefully entering a significant location and not leaving for an extended period of time. The location might be a politician's office, a government building, the offices of a company that is worsening the problem, a park, a street, or any location that is of importance to the issue. A sit-in can take place both legally and illegally, depending on whether you have permission to be in the location and whether it is public or private property.

Sit-down: Similar to a sit-in, a sit-down involves sitting *outside* a location rather than inside. This typically suits larger sized groups, simply because there are fewer logistical challenges involved.

Vigil: This form of gathering is used to recognise and protest the suffering of an individual or group; in particular, to grieve deaths that have occurred by unjust means. A vigil will often be silent, or with just a few speakers, and have a far more solemn tone than a regular protest. Vigils often take place in the evening with attendees holding candles or other small light sources, although this is not always the case. Vigils are highly emotional events, and it's vital to approach the topic in a sensitive and respectful way.

Picket: Most commonly used during strikes in the labour union movement, picketing is the process of standing or walking around outside a significant location, such as a workplace entrance during a strike, or a business during a boycott, holding signs to show what you're fighting for. Pickets can last whole days, weeks, months or even longer, particularly during a strike or occupation.

Secret and unannounced actions: When done well, the surprise event is a great tool in activism. Often performed illegally, and organised by a pre-planned group of people, these are some of the most exciting to see happen and can work best to heighten public awareness of a problem. The organising process generally involves extensive legal briefings and preparation, so that participants are fully aware of their rights and the potential risks they are exposing themselves to. The most common example of an unannounced event is a sitin, although there can be more extreme forms of action, such as blocking roads, scaling or locking yourself to buildings or equipment, or large-scale occupations of places that last for an extended period of time.

Step 2: Time to organise

A common mistake made by first-time organisers is not allowing yourself enough time to pull together an event. When you first start planning, it's easy to get ahead of yourself by skimming over details and running straight into the more 'fun' parts of organising. However, you'll find there's a lot of important work to get done, and it's always best to allow yourself as much (if not more) time as is needed to complete it all.

To figure out how much time you need, it's super helpful to create a **Gantt chart,** a spreadsheet commonly used in the management of big projects. Start off by creating a list of every job that needs to get done. You might have some tasks that aren't covered here, depending on the group you're working with and the different circumstances surrounding your event, but this guide should cover most essential roles. It's important to note that the larger any event grows, the more specific and unusual the roles that pop up will be. I've worked on Gantts before that had 30 rows, and others with nearly 200 rows.

Once you have this list, separate it into different sections according to whether the job needs to be done before the event, on the day, or afterwards. Depending on the number of tasks, you might also choose to separate them into further categories, such as 'promotion', 'logistics' or 'media'. These are then placed in one column of a spreadsheet, with other columns for who is to take on the task, when it needs to be completed by, and whether it's been completed. The Gantt is set out in rows with week-by-week check-ins to see how jobs are progressing. A simple Gantt might look like this:

Task	Who	To be completed by	Week 1	Week 2	Week 3	Day of	Afterwards
Printing posters		Week 2					
Contacting police		Week 1					
Briefing marshalls		Day of					
Sending thank-you emails		Afterwards					
Organising Welcome to Country		Week 2					
Locking in speakers/performers		Week 3					

Once you've created this base Gantt, hold a team meeting to assign roles to ensure all tasks will be completed. It's useful to consider which tasks should be done by the same person based on whether they intersect (such as thank-you emails being sent by the same person who contacted speakers and performers), and to make sure people aren't overloaded with tasks that are due at the same time. With every following meeting, keep track of how far you've progressed by running through the Gantt, colour-coding the squares and adding notes to show how tasks are progressing.

Once completed, your Gantt should look a little like this:

Task	Who	To be complete by:	Week 1	Week 2	Week 3	Day of	Afterwards
Printing posters	Dani	Week 2	Poster design edited, printer contacted	All printed and distributed			
Contacting police	Riley	Week 1	Form 1 submitted	Confirmed details and permissions			
Briefing marshalls	Meg	Day of		Waiting for confirmed logistical details	Plan made		
Sending thank-you emails	Parker	Afterwards				Draft written	Sent out
Organising Welcome to Country	Dani	Week 2	Reached out to elders	Confirming payment			
Locking in speakers/ performers	Parker	Week 3		Reached out to potential speakers/ local bands	All fully confirmed, logistical details passed on		

Key : ■ Not yet started ■ Underway ■ Finished

Creating your Gantt should make it much easier to figure out how much time you'll need to pull the event together. This, again, will vary, depending on the amount of people on your team and the capacity they have. If you're organising your first event, or most of your team are new to activism and learning as they go, I'd recommend allowing at least a month to organise, although several months would be better. This might be a tight timeline, but sometimes you don't even have this much time to organise. You might be planning what is referred to as a 'snap action' – a protest that is planned quickly to react to an event, and takes place in the short period when public interest in the topic is high. Sometimes these have to be put together in one or two days, or over a couple of weeks. In order for these events to be successful, they need as many people involved as possible to ensure all tasks can be finished quickly – and some steps might need to be skipped.

Step 3: Pick the date

Be tactical in planning the date of your protest–
- Is the day meaningful for some reason?
- Is it the first sitting day of parliament?

- Will leaders be voting on policy close to that date?
- Will it be a time when people are particularly motivated to act? (For example, on climate change at the end of a summer of bushfires.)

If you choose a meaningful date to protest, people will see more reason to get involved. However, this is not 100 per cent necessary for a successful action. And it's extremely important to check whether there's another important event happening on the date you've chosen – you don't want there to be any unforeseen distractions or 'competitors' on the day. Look out in advance for notable dates, such as significant religious events or major sporting games. It's also worthwhile considering any particular barriers for those attending, for example, NAPLAN or an exam period for school students. Additionally, it's sensible to look up the date on Facebook and other sites to see if any large events are scheduled for that day. If you find there's a similar protest action taking place on the same date, it's worthwhile reaching out to the organisers to see how you could collaborate or liaise to ensure you're both as successful as possible.

Step 4: Pick the time

When deciding on the time for an event, it's important to consider a variety of factors. If you're planning the event on a weekday, it's generally best to hold it after work/school hours, so that you can maximise attendance. If you're in a central location near plenty of workplaces, any time around 5.30pm will work well. However, if it's being held at a location for a specific reason, such as outside a parliament building while politicians debate a particular policy, it might need to be earlier in the day.

Additionally, the time of day can help with the visuals being created – an after-dark event allows for extensive use of light-based imagery from sources such as candles, projectors and coloured torches.

However, if you're planning to hold an event during the middle of the day (similar to the climate strikes) so that people will have to skip school or work, this in itself can create a massive statement. Bear in mind, though, that this does make attending far more difficult for most people. If you're planning an event at a weekend, midday to early evening is best – that way, people don't need to wake up too early and it will end at a time that isn't wildly late.

Step 5: Choose the location

In choosing a location, the number one thing you should be considering is accessibility. Ensure the space is fully accessible by wheelchairs or other mobility devices; this primarily includes having pathways at least a meter wide, and gentle slopes both in the space itself and the surrounding area. There should be (ideally multiple) accessible bathrooms nearby, which have adequate space and a metal transfer pole. Additionally, there should be shaded areas both near the centre of the action and in a more quiet spot. If there's seating already available that's particularly helpful, though if not it's possible to create sitting areas with your own resources, such as fold-out chairs.

The potential size of whatever action you're planning will dictate the locations you need to consider. Predicting the number of people who will attend an event is a really tricky thing. If you have an RSVP system (such as for a Facebook event), a good rule of thumb is that about a third to half of the people who respond will end up attending. You can gain a rough idea from the amount of interest and buzz about the protest before the day, but ultimately, until the event happens, you can never know. Once you've organised a few actions, you'll be able to determine more accurately how many you expect to come along, based on prior success and patterns of attendance.

Unless you're targeting a specific building or place, you should aim to be in a central area where you'll be noticed. Look for a space that is large enough to comfortably fit a lot of people, yet small enough to create an impactful image. It can be helpful to look up previous protests and general events that have taken place in the area to help you gauge the capacity of various places, while also noting if there are 'iconic' or often-used protest spots. Ensure that it's easily accessible – near a train station or bus stop is ideal. The area should be flat enough to hold a stage, if that's what you want; however, a gentle hill shouldn't be much of an issue.

An important consideration is whether you'll be on public or private property. If it's private property, you need to know whether you'll be able to stay there for an extended period of time. Make sure to look into this thoroughly – you can often discover that areas such as parks are under private ownership, meaning you need to contact the owners to ensure you're able to host an event there. Even when you've found a location you like, be sure to plan a couple of back-up spots as well. Ideally you'll be able to hold the event at your first-choice location, but do plan for the possibility that it won't be available.

It's always tricky to choose your location when you don't know exactly how many people will attend your event. As well as planning as comprehensively as you can, you need to be prepared to think on your feet and make decisions on the day. During the bushfire crisis of early 2020, Uni Students for Climate Justice along with Extinction Rebellion organised 'Sack ScoMo' rallies and marches across Australia, leaving themselves only about 10 days to do so. I helped marshall the event held in Sydney, and I knew many of my friends were coming along as well.

On the day, the other marshalls and I underwent a briefing, at which we were told the estimated turnout was 'all over the place', but might reach 30,000 people if it went really well. At the time I thought this was an incredibly over-optimistic goal – despite there being a lot of interest on Facebook, I assumed not nearly as many would actually show up. As protestors started arriving, I began to ask the crowd who had gathered outside the wrong area to 'Please move around the corner into Town Hall Square'. Then I had to start yelling the instructions.

> **SUDDENLY I WAS OVERWHELMED BY A FLOOD OF PEOPLE; THERE WERE THOUSANDS SHOWING UP BY THE MINUTE WITH NO SIGN OF IT SLOWING DOWN.**

I continued scrambling through and yelling at the crowd, approaching stationary groups and gesturing madly while following my script of 'Please move down around the corner into Town Hall Square. Yep, down in this direction and then right at the corner; *that's* where the rally is being held! That's *this* direction! *This direction!*'

As my phone had died earlier that day (massive rookie error – don't ever leave home on the day of a protest without a charging bank!), I had almost no means of getting in touch with the other marshalls and organisers, so I had to go with my gut. I continued the process of directing protestors the right way, which due to the sheer volume of people was growing increasingly more difficult. When I finally caught sight of the yellow vest of another marshall, I ran over and asked what the hell was going on. I was told that, while I'd been effective in gathering people to the right area, there wasn't much point in doing that now as there was no space whatsoever left for people to cram into.

The streets surrounding the building were filled with people, and there was a queue of banked-up buses (also filled with people) right behind us.

We managed to find another couple of our friends who were marshalling and tried to communicate with police as to how we should approach the situation. However, at that point there was very little we could do. After getting word that more help was needed on stage (the front steps of Town Hall), I ended up sprinting around the block to the back of the protest, then up a little-used side entrance into the square, and snaked my way through the waves of people and up onto the stage.

We were asked to ensure that everyone on the stage was either a speaker or organiser who needed to be there; there was soon to be a demonstration by Extinction Rebellion 'Red Rebels' on the stairs, so the whole space needed to be clear. This was a chaotic job – for every person we asked to walk back down the stairs, another would walk up. Eventually, however, we were able to make the space less hectic – except for one particular man. He was standing with his arms crossed and large sunglasses resting on his face, and was clearly a member of the public. I approached him and asked if there was any reason for him to be up at the front. After ignoring me a couple of times, he finally answered that he was 'working'. I asked who he was working with, to which he responded, 'None ya business'. Again, I stated that unless he had a purpose for being there he needed to head back down. I had noticed that he smelt strongly of marijuana and was clearly aggravated by my questioning, so I asked an adult marshall to step in to try to help out. Surprise, surprise: he stayed put. Over the next 20 minutes we tried to slowly edge him out of the space by moving ever closer to him, but it didn't help much. Panic started to set in as the Red Rebels were about to perform and he had still not left. Miraculously, however, he headed down just in time to not disrupt the demonstration.

At last, the time came for us to march from Town Hall. Due to the chaos of the rally so far, we were running about an hour behind schedule, meaning that some groups of people were already starting to disperse. The vast majority chose to stick around, however, resulting in an enormous march. I spent almost all my time instructing people to 'Please stay on the road! *On the road!*', which would work for brief periods before everyone started spreading out onto the pavement again. At one point we suddenly ground to a complete halt and were still for a while; everyone was confused as to what was going on. We discovered that the head of the march had met the tail, as the route crossed itself at an intersection. While we were stopped, the crowd claimed the stairs that stretched across the front of a large corner office building and held at least a couple of thousand protesters. We danced, chanted and generally made as much noise as possible until we were allowed to start moving again.

Eventually, I reached the very front of the march, and to an extent gave up my marshalling duties so I could take part in the protest. I felt the familiar soreness in my throat, pain in my calf muscles and all-consuming agony in my feet. (Another cautionary note: it never works out well if you wear platform Doc Martens to rallies.)

But, as always, I loved every moment of it. The march came to a close, the protestors slowly dispersed, the adrenaline that had sustained my body the entire time began to fade, and I soon became aware of just how exhausted I actually was.

Step 6: Decide on the march route

A march is a powerful and impactful part of many protests.

> **WHILE PASSIONATE SPEAKERS AT A RALLY CREATE INSPIRATIONAL MOMENTS, HAVING EVERYONE TAKE PART IN ONE CENTRALISED ACTIVITY CREATES A UNIQUELY ENORMOUS DISPLAY OF PEOPLE-POWER.**

And, of course, a march is a super-fun part of an event, makes sure that no one can miss you.

If you choose to hold a march from your original rally location, plan a route to pass through main streets and central areas that will be seen by heaps of people. The route should be fully accessible. This means pathways wide enough for wheelchair use, no barriers or obstacles in the way, no steep slopes, and nothing too exerting. On the day, it can be useful to create designated rest spots with sitting areas during the march, which attendees are made aware of before they start moving. You should be able to walk the route in about 10–15 minutes at a regular pace (you'll find your pace will be much slower during the actual event). Any less and it might feel too brief and curtailed, but much longer can lead to overtiredness and a loss of enthusiasm, and there are few things as underwhelming as a quiet and bored march. However, this most certainly isn't gospel – and if you think a different length would be better for your particular event, then go for it.

Once you've planned a route, take time to walk it out to pinpoint areas that could be of concern (where the road narrows, or you march through a quiet location with few people, and so on). Think about the elements you want to include. Do you want to end back at your starting point or gather at a secondary location? Going back to the starting point will give you access to your main equipment again, which can make things easier to formally finish; however, this can cause some concerns in very large groups because the front of the march can meet up with the tail end. Finishing at a different point, however, can make it more difficult to communicate that the march has ended – typically you won't have access to a speaker system as large as the one at your gathering point, and it might not feel as circular and 'complete'. But it does give you the opportunity to end at a significant location. Finishing at a politician's office, parliamentary location, company office that doesn't align with your goals, or any other point of significance, can definitely help in further identifying what you're fighting against. It also gives more excitement and dynamism to the event. If you can't finish outside an important place, you can always walk past it or stop outside on the way to your final destination.

After deciding on your route, work out whether you want to stay on the pavement or take up the road (smaller events can work quite well on the pavement, but as you begin to grow, the road space is often necessary). Sometimes the prospect of taking up the space of a road can be appealing and exciting for organisers – totally understandable, but it isn't always super effective.

Remember: a small group spread out sparsely across a large area almost always looks less impressive than that same group crowded into a smaller area.

It's also worth considering the importance of the statement of blocking a road and disrupting 'business as usual' for your cause – often this statement alone can be just as important as the march itself.

Once you've finalised your plan for a route, it's a good idea to come up with a couple of alternatives to fall back on, in case your main route isn't approved. If you have to move to Plan B, be clear which elements of the route you deem necessary, and which could be dropped.

Step 7: Get approval

Once you've decided on your rally location and/or proposed march route, you can choose to get in contact with the police so that your event can take place legally. This will make the process of organising easier in many ways, and largely removes the risk of your event being shut down or attendees being arrested or fined.

The first step is to file a 'Notice of Intention to Hold a Public Assembly' or 'Form 1' (this form might have a slightly different name depending on your state). You'll typically need to submit this a minimum of 4–7 days before the event, although this could vary depending on where you live. On the form, you'll need to fill in a whole heap of details about your event, such as the start and finish times, estimated turnout, whether you're having any musical performances, and if you've planned a 'procession' (a fancy word for march). You'll also give the details of a member of your group who will be your assigned 'police liaison', and who will stay in contact with police in the lead-up to, and during, the event. Once you've submitted the form, within a few days you should receive information as to whether it's been approved, or perhaps some elements they would like you to adjust. You might need to negotiate with police to get to your desired outcome – this might feel a bit daunting. If you do need to negotiate, try to explain to the police the importance of the particular part of the event they're trying to change, and see if you can reach a compromise.

> **SOMETIMES YOU NEED TO HOLD YOUR GROUND; JUST BECAUSE YOU'RE A YOUNG PERSON DOESN'T MEAN YOU SHOULDN'T BE TREATED SERIOUSLY.**

While you can be diligent and firm during this process, remember to stay calm and reasonable; ultimately you want this negotiation to be as smooth and effective as possible. Unfortunately, though, you might find the police will not allow certain elements you've proposed, no matter how much you contest them. If you're in this position, revert to your back-up plans, move forward and adjust quickly to the setback.

Step 8: Get council approval

Depending on your location, you might have to apply for council approval – this varies messily between states. In the Northern Territory on public roads and in some public areas, and in some parts of Victoria, it's essential you have a permit from your local council *and* police to hold a protest. In South Australia, you can choose to apply for approval from either the police *or* your council. In Queensland, it's generally recommended that you submit a notice of intention to hold a public assembly to your local council; however, it's not 100 per cent necessary. And in New South Wales, ACT and Western Australia, council approval is *not* necessary. To be completely sure, get in touch with your local council to check if a permit/approval is required.

The information required on the form can also vary depending on your location. Typically, it will be similar to the police form, but on some occasions you might need to submit a risk assessment and/or proof of insurance. Different councils and areas have different requirements for the risk assessment, which should be detailed on their websites. Additionally, if you're required to give proof of insurance and you don't have any, a sensible option is to reach out to another group that has insurance. A lot of officialised community groups and non-government organisations have public liability insurance; get in touch with a group you've previously worked with, or who is helping pull the event together, and ask if you could use their insurance for the event.

Step 9: Promote the event

To make sure people hear all about your event *before* it takes place, it's vital to start promoting early. You can find a bunch of useful tactics for this in Chapter 6. The initial push of promotion should have the main goals of letting people know the date of the event and educating them further about the issue you're protesting against. Make sure to send this information to any people who gave you their contact details at earlier events, and encourage them to continue sharing it. As you get closer to the date, be sure to ramp up the promotion, shifting your messaging to emphasise the time and location.

The final few days before a rally are the most important in determining the turnout, as people are far more likely to make concrete plans to attend. This is why it's important to not oversaturate with promotion too far from the date, or people will grow bored by the time the date rolls around. Try to send emails to your base every day or two during the week leading up to the event, and regularly update social media pages to generate further excitement. At this stage, it's key to constantly be spreading the details for the event and encouraging all those planning to attend to share the information with those around them. In these last few days, you should be able to make a rough estimate of your potential turnout. Try not to be too specific if you choose to promote this; for example, always state that you're anticipating 'hundreds' of people, rather than '500–600'.

Step 10: Brief the media

It's important to send out a press release to your contacts early on, to help get the word out to other potential attendees via the media. The statement should include the date and time of the rally, why it's important, what your aims are, and a couple of quotes from organisers. (For more information on this, see the press release in Chapter 9.)

You should send out another press release during the final few days before the event.

Step 11: Welcome to Country

I cannot stress enough how important it is to have a Welcome to Country at every major event. This is an address given by an Aboriginal or Torres Strait Islander elder, welcoming those in attendance to their land and giving them safe passage. As all land in a colonised world is stolen from the traditional custodians, at any gathering it's vital that this is addressed and discussed. Indigenous people are at the forefront of a great variety of social issues, largely in part to inherited trauma and still-present racism experienced by Indigenous peoples spanning back to the beginning of colonisation.

> **HAVING A WELCOME TO COUNTRY SHOWS YOUR COMMITMENT TO ALL FORMS OF JUSTICE AND IS AN INTEGRAL PART OF THE PROCESS OF ENSURING YOUR ACTIVISM IS INTERSECTIONAL.**

If possible, at your venue, you could look into having a smoking ceremony – an ancient Aboriginal custom that involves the burning of native plants, the smoke of which cleanses the space and wards off bad spirits.

You usually need to book a Welcome to Country in advance and pay a speaker fee. Depending on your area, you'll have to request this through different Indigenous land councils and groups. If there isn't an option on their website, simply send an email asking for direction.

If you're unable to confirm an official Welcome to Country, due to time or availability constraints or other issues, an Acknowledgement of Country is suitable. This can be delivered by any person, Indigenous or not, and is an acknowledgement of the traditional owners of the land you're meeting on and an extension of respect to all Indigenous people and leaders present. You're probably familiar with this already – it's typically read out at school assemblies and many other gatherings. Look up online which land the meeting will be on, and who are the local custodians. The general template for an Acknowledgement of Country is: 'I would like to begin by acknowledging the <insert name> people, Traditional Custodians of the land on which we gather today, and pay my respects to their Elders past and present. I extend that respect to Aboriginal and Torres Strait Islander peoples here today.' You can change this format to be a little more specific; often it aids to mention that the land itself was stolen, and that sovereignty was never ceded.

Step 12: Find speakers

Choosing the right speakers for the day is an important part of organising a rally. Not only do the speakers reflect the movement itself, but they often provide the main 'takeaways' people receive from the event. So, how do you choose them?

Try brainstorming the impacts of your issue on different people and communities. Think about who is suffering the most. From this, make a draft plan of the types of speakers you'd like to have on the day.

Make a conscious effort to share stories that you think deserve to be elevated, and to prioritise marginalised and less privileged voices and those that are rarely represented. You're creating a large platform to mobilise and educate people, so use the opportunity wisely.

If you simply retell the same narrative from the same perspectives that are seen all the time, what is the value of highlighting these stories at all? Not only would you be rehashing the same mainstream image, but you wouldn't be providing a clear and holistic vision of the issue and the ways in which it impacts people.

Direct-action events are an opportunity like no other, when you can choose to uplift the voices that aren't heard enough in front of an audience that is willing to engage and learn.

To make sure you're showing the whole picture, include a diverse range of ages, genders, abilities, ethnic backgrounds (in particular Black and Indigenous People of Colour), economic classes, geographic backgrounds and so on.

For example, if you were organising a protest about safe and equitable access to abortion, perhaps your draft speaker plan might be:

- a doctor, to discuss the importance of safe access to abortion and the risks of home procedures
- someone who had an abortion as a teenager, to explain their experience
- an Aboriginal person to discuss the inequalities in health-care access
- a transgender man or non-binary person who has had an abortion, discussing the importance of inclusive language and intesectionality
- someone who nearly died or had severe complications from an unsafe home abortion, or someone who lost or nearly lost a friend or relative to one

This list provides a set of stories from different walks of life, ensuring a more diverse and interesting picture about the importance of community access to safe abortion than is often depicted in the mainstream. You might choose to have a less ambitious plan, depending on time constraints and the amount of pre-existing contacts you have; or you might be in an area where it's difficult to find a diverse array of speakers.

Depending on the length of your event, the number of speakers you need will vary. Plan to have speakers or performers presenting for about 75 per cent of the time your event is planned to run for. This allows wriggle room for the introductions and a buffer between each person, and also accounts for the tendency for speakers to go over time due to frequent pauses as the crowd responds. You should ask speakers to talk for 3–5 minutes each, and make sure to stress the importance of keeping to time. (Even with all this planning, it often feels impossible for any rally keep to time.)

Once you've decided who you would *like* to speak, the time comes to actually find these people. This can be a difficult task, so start early. As a team, have a discussion to see if anybody has contacts that fit the bill. Then try reaching out through a number of different means. If you want to get in touch with a particular worker of some type it's a good idea to contact unions or campaign groups made up of individuals in that area (such as Doctors for the Environment).

You can also reach out to allies and other groups within your movement to see if they have any members who would be suitable and willing to speak. If you've someone particular in mind, even just sending them a direct message on social media can be enough to get the ball rolling. Chatting with friends and family to see if they have any contacts is also often surprisingly helpful. Additionally, if there is enough interest, you could have an open form for people to apply to speak.

During this process, it's somewhat unlikely that you'll find someone to match every slot in your draft plan, and that's totally okay. There are bound to be lots of other people with unique and interesting stories to tell who would also be great for your purpose – it's just a matter of talking to people and exploring different networks to bring together a good list.

As you make contact with these potential speakers, it's good to have a template invitation email ready to send. If you haven't been in touch with them before, begin with a short paragraph about yourself and the sort of work you do. This doesn't need to go into too much detail, but should provide them with a solid understanding of who you are and what your group stands for. Then discuss the event itself and its importance, and what you are hoping to achieve. Describe the event in a way that does it justice, and shows why they should be excited about it. Now tell them where they come into the picture! Ask if they'd like to speak on the day, and let them know what they would be discussing (if there's something in particular you have in mind). If they choose to confirm, make sure to thank them before writing down their phone number or another form of communication to keep in case of technical issues, and then continue to keep them in the loop as the event approaches. If they don't wish to be involved or aren't able to speak, make sure to let them know it's completely okay and thank them for their time.

On the day, having a live Auslan interpreter allows for these speeches to be accessible to everyone. This can be booked online, through a collection of different service providers. If you're livestreaming your event, organising live captioning is also useful.

Step 13: Choose an MC

Typically at a rally-style event, someone (usually two people) acts as master of ceremonies (MC). Their role is to 'host' the rally, by introducing speakers and ensuring attendees are aware of what's going on at all times. They should be enthusiastic and confident public speakers, able to think on their feet and adjust quickly; often the MCs will be organisers of the event or people who are active within the movement. They might give a speech at the beginning or during the event, and host activities and calls to action throughout.

A rally led by MCs will usually follow a general structure; however, feel free to shake this up as much as you'd like. To begin with, the MCs will briefly introduce themselves, where they're from and what sort of work they do, before passing over to the Elder who is delivering the Welcome to Country (even if you do shake up the order, this should always be delivered as early as possible). After thanking the Elder, the MCs will make some opening remarks before delivering the housekeeping and logistical information to the crowd (everyone move forwards towards the stage; there are first-aid staff over here, and so on.).

They will then describe the issue the rally is focused on and why it's important, along with the demands of the event. The first MC might discuss the issue at hand, while the second discusses the solutions and what needs to be done. These speeches are best kept short and punchy: while informative, they're mainly to motivate the crowd and generate an emotive response, so ensure the script is passionate with several poignant and powerful lines.

Once this is done, the MCs will start moving through the rest of the program. This will often consist of alternating between welcoming a speaker or performer to the stage, and thanking them once they have finished. At various moments throughout the program, the MCs might have a couple of breaks to lead chants and other activities to help pump up the crowd, and repeatedly explain all calls to actions and demands. They will also update the crowd of any important information throughout the event. If there's going to be a march at the end of the event, they will instruct everyone where to exit, and what route will be taken. Finally, before the march proceeds or at the end of the rally, they'll thank everyone for attending and finish on a final 'pump up' or call to action.

I've been an MC a few times since I became an activist. I think one of the strangest – but also most fun – events was a joint School Strike 4 Climate and #StopAdani protest, held outside Anthony Albanese's office a few weeks before the 2019 election. Unlike at previous school strikes, we chose to hold multiple events in every location, primarily targeting MPs' offices. We wanted to show that neither major party had a climate policy that would actually be of significance, and place as much pressure as possible on our politicians to implement deep and meaningful climate policy before the election rolled around.

Our first plan was to hold a sit-in inside Albanese's office, but we soon received word that he's a master at ignoring protestors.

> **WE REALISED WE'D NEED TO FIND A WAY TO BE MASSIVELY DIFFICULT TO BRUSH OFF, AND MAKE OURSELVES ANNOYINGLY IMPOSSIBLE TO IGNORE.**

We came up with the idea of a 'musical sit-in' – we'd hand out kazoos and boomwhackers to the crowd and hold a karaoke-style event. Now, I can't begin to tell you the stress involved in ordering hundreds of kazoos just a couple of days before an event – particularly when a volunteer treks out for an hour to pick them up and it turns out they're out of stock, but didn't say so on the order! We somehow managed to acquire a hundred or so kazoos the day before the sit-in.

As we pulled up to his office, we immediately noticed that there was no way we'd all fit into the space. I had heard beforehand that it was small, but I hadn't anticipated just how exceptionally tiny it was. We quickly decided we'd have to stay outside, so we set up a stage of about eight milk crates hastily strung together with zip ties and plugged our speaker into the shop next door. Over the next 30 minutes or so, streams of kids began rocking up. We handed out kazoo after kazoo until there were none left, and still hordes of people were piling into the area. By the time the rally was ready to start, the tiny sheltered walkway and driveway surrounding the office was jam-packed. It was chaos, and I took my place on the milk-crate stage and began the proceedings.

We'd asked for suggestions on Instagram for a playlist that everyone could sing and kazoo along to, and posted the lyrics online. I was attempting to both energise the crowd and blast the kazoo, leading to it nearly flying out of my mouth on too many occasions. It was a weird yet fun event, with everyone tooting along to their heart's content. That is, until it started raining. It crept up on us in unassuming sprinkles, before properly pouring down. Probably about half of those in attendance decided to leave at this moment, as our speaker had turned off and they were stuck, standing around, uncomfortable and damp.

Despite this, we felt the show must go on and we continued our musical tirade. It grew more chaotic by the second, as more and more people attempted to crowd into the sheltered section, eventually opening the floodgates into the office itself. A couple of dozen students squeezed themselves into a room that was designed to hold five at most. They were chanting, jumping, singing and (most importantly) kazooing. It was pure, beautiful mayhem.

Step 14: The call to action

One of the most important parts of any protest or rally is the 'call to action'. This is the point at which something is directly asked of attendees, which allows them to continue their action long after the event has officially finished. This might be asking them to call a particular MP every day for a week, or attend a similar rally held by another group, donate to an important cause, start a conversation, or join a new campaign. A call to action should be something that everyone can reasonably commit to in the moment, and have the ability to continue doing after the day. No matter what you choose as your call to action, ensure the wording is clear and that it's a task everyone in the crowd will either be able to take part in during the moment, or be able to hear and act on later.

Step 15: Create a program

Structuring a well-thought-out program is necessary for any successful day of action. Once you've decided on the MCs and the exact number of speakers and performers for the day, create a schedule to ensure everything goes smoothly and everyone is on the same page. The schedule should go into quite a bit of depth, with all important times and tasks listed. Include other columns for every *When*, *What* and *Who*, so that everyone is fully aware what's happening at all times and at what times they are needed. Part of the difficulty in creating a schedule for a rally is that you can't truly rehearse what will happen on the day and how long everything will take. However, to the best of your ability, on the day try to keep to the times on the schedule.

When	What	Who
2 hours before	Set-up event	Set-up crew
1 hour before	Marshall/first aid briefing	Marshalls, first aid
Start time	People arriving; marshalls lead everyone in	Marshalls
10 mins in	Welcome to Country	Elder
20 mins in	MCs welcome	MCs
25 mins in	Speeches Part 1	First 2–3 speakers
40 mins in	Performances	Performers
50 mins in	Speeches Part 2	Final 2–3 speakers
65 mins in	Call to action	MCs
75 mins in	Explain march	MCs
80 mins in	March	Marshalls
110 mins in	March end, MCs thank you and wrap-up	MCs
140 mins in	Pack-down	Pack-down crew

If you have a speaker or performer who stays on stage for much longer than their allocated time, it can be very awkward trying to get them to finish so the event can continue and the timing can get back on track. Agree beforehand on a sign or gesture you can make from the side of the stage to remind them they need to finish speaking soon, such as a raised arm or '5 minutes' gesture.

Step 16: Get wired for sound

Depending on your expected turnout, you'll need a public address (PA) system – a fancy way of saying a speaker system. These can vary wildly in size. Remember that it's always better to get a system that is slightly too large than one that's too small; otherwise, people at the back of the crowd might not be able to hear anything. It's always best to overestimate your potential turnout when looking into equipment; cater for more, rather than less. You'll also need to organise a power source for the PA. Sometimes local buildings will allow you to plug into their source, but the majority of the time you'll need to hire a battery. Again, the size of this will vary depending on how large your speaker system is and how long the speakers will need to last. It can be helpful to reach out to local organisations and other allies to see if you can borrow their equipment; many will be willing to help and support you. Or you can rent a system; however, this can be expensive, so get a lot of quotes and try to find a rental service that will offer you a discount, or potentially pro-bono support. Before the day, make sure you're aware of your power source, any need for extension cords and, if you're having performers, how they can link their electric instrument (such as a keyboard or guitar) to the system.

Step 17: Set the stage

A stage is essential at almost every gathering so that speakers can actually be seen and so that there's a definite area for people to be watching. The best sort of stage is one that's integrated into the space itself, such as the steps of a town hall, or a natural hill or elevated area in a park or at the front of a building. However, most of the time this isn't an option. For smaller events, a stack of milk crates works perfectly well as a stage. If you choose this option, make sure to bring a bunch of cable ties and string so that you can tie the crates together and ensure the 'stage' is secure. If you're holding a larger event, where a milk-crate stage won't be high or wide enough, try reaching out to local NGOs and community groups to see if anyone has a small portable stage you could borrow. If you have the budget, it might be worthwhile renting a stage for the day. Always be aware if any of the speakers have accessibility issues, and adjust the space accordingly. This should include a gentle ramp onto the stage, and ensuring the stage is large enough for safe ease of access.

Step 18: Signal your intent – banners and props

Create a strong visual element or further point of interest at your event with signs, banners and props. They might provide an exciting photo opportunity, emphasise the point of the action, or create a place where people can interact. For example, during a sit-down outside the Liberal Party's Sydney headquarters in November 2019, we handed out pens and small rectangular strips of fabric to the crowd on which to write messages to the party. Everyone wrote their message, then passed their strip back to the front of the event to be hung on a long length of rope. We ended up with hundreds of these messages strung up, creating a strong visual of the people-power present at the event, in addition to making an aesthetically appealing image.

Another example was during an anti-gas mobilisation held during the COVID-19 pandemic. We spent countless hours painting over 100 placards, each with different designs and colours. We then clipped these to makeshift 'washing lines', which were constructed from poles with holes drilled in them, through which rope could be threaded. We spread them out across our space, then placed a group of socially distanced strikers among them. This worked as a backdrop to a press conference we held, providing visual interest while also representing the vast numbers of people who couldn't mobilise due to public safety concerns. Consider all the different ways design elements could be used; the more creative and interesting, the better.

In the lead-up to an event, to help generate excitement at the same time as ensuring there's a variety of interesting signs and banners, you can organise a 'crafternoon'. This is an event in itself where people make a whole heap of signs and props that can be handed out on the day. See if any local groups can donate their space to you for an afternoon for this to happen, otherwise local church halls, parks, an organiser's house, or communal areas work well (remember to get permission, if necessary). These events often are relatively small and informal, so word of mouth and a few posts on social media should be enough to get the word out.

Before the day, stock up on old cardboard, plastic political placards, or any other materials you can use to make signs. Long sheets of canvas or other fabrics are very useful for making banners. Make sure you have lots of different paint colours and brushes for people to use. You can ask attendees to bring materials, but you should have enough if not many do. If you're trying to make a larger banner, it is helpful to have a projector. Pin up a large sheet of fabric, project the text you want onto it, then trace its outline lightly with pencils. Transfer the fabric back onto the floor and paint in the lines.

People can then either take their posters home with them, or, even better, you can store them all and hand them out on the day. Not only do these craft events create useful resources for the day, but they also help generate buzz around the main event and get more people involved.

Step 19: First aid and safety

The amount of first aid support you need will depend on the weather and the size of the event. On a particularly warm day, people attending a rally are at risk of dehydration and overheating, which can occasionally cause them to pass out. Standing out in the sun for a few hours can easily cause sunstroke or burning. Make sure to have a first aid table set up with plenty of water and other necessary supplies, along with one or two volunteers with first aid qualifications to help out. If you're planning a large event, you might want to pay for first aid attendance by an official service, such as St John Ambulance. They can provide medical assistance on the day, meaning that if anything serious does happen with somebody's health, they'll be in the hands of medical professionals.

Step 20: Brief the marshalls

Particularly if you're organising a march, crowd marshalls are extremely important. Their role is to ensure people understand what's happening, help protestors feel safe and comfortable, and to help with crowd control and anything else that might pop up. They should be given a briefing from an experienced marshall, referred to as the 'head marshall' (likely to be the most experienced and confident marshall among your volunteers), about an hour before the event begins. This brief should outline where people will be coming in, the march route, the end location, where to direct people, the location of water/bathrooms/first aid, anyone's specific responsibilities, and anything else relevant to the event.

Marshalls should also be briefed on how to stay calm when dealing with people who might act aggressively, identifying people who may need medical assistance, and generally ensuring people feel comfortable. Make sure to provide a uniform of sorts for the marshalls on the day – a high-visibility vest is one of the best options as it's easy to spot from a distance. Try to get your hands on some high-quality walkie talkies for the marshalls and organisers; these are a godsend during an enormous event as phones run out of charge so quickly and, once crowds reach into the tens of thousands, phone lines often stop working.

Step 21: Organise photographers and videographers

It's a sad truth these days that if there aren't any photos or videos of an event, did it even happen? Make sure to get your event documented. Before the day, lock in several photographers to take high-quality images, which they have agreed for you to use for free afterwards, during the event. They don't need to be professional photographers; some of my favourite shots of school strikes have been taken by teenagers who brought along a camera on the day. Make sure to have a Google Drive or Dropbox set up beforehand that the photographers are aware of, so that all the images can be easily stored and found in one place. Additionally, by letting attendees know to use a particular hashtag and asking them to tag your social media when posting photos, you'll gain access to a massive bank of images.

Step 22: Keep people involved

Once people have attended an event, you want them to stay engaged afterwards. This will allow you to have consistent communication and let them know ways in which they can become more involved in the movement. This also means you'll build a network so you don't need to start afresh trying to reach people every time you hold an action; rather, you can directly contact your network and let them know your upcoming plans.

To collect people's details at small rallies, have several clipboards with sign-up sheets ready, while at larger events you'll need tech infrastructure, such as text-in numbers. This is often overlooked but it's super important in ensuring your network continues to grow and people know how to stay involved. Make it clear what they will gain by signing up, with statements such as 'text this number to receive updates on upcoming events, campaigns and volunteering opportunities'.

Once the event has come to a close, it's time to flood both social and traditional media with images and news of what just happened. Email another press release that includes the turnout and any interesting information from the day, as well as the details of who to contact for more information.

Step 23: Say thank you

Now, this is the step I'm guilty of forgetting far too often, which makes me feel like quite the undignified, bad-mannered child. Often, when you get caught up in all the chaos and excitement at the end of an event, you forget some of the little things that need to be done *after* the day. If you were the main point of contact for a speaker or performer, be sure to send an email expressing your gratitude to them for choosing to help out and be part of what made the day so great. Additionally, take the time to genuinely thank everyone who helped pull the event together.

Step 24: Debrief

Congratulations: you've pulled off a direct action! After any sort of action, debriefing is enormously important. It allows space for reflection and growth, which will help you consistently improve as organisers. If possible, it's best to debrief in person. Take time to congratulate the group on holding a protest, make sure you recognise the importance of your achievements and how your efforts have paid off. Then, as a group, start to discuss what went well, ensuring that everyone has an opportunity to speak. Then, discuss what could have gone better. After each person has made their point, it's helpful to discuss as a team whether others agree with the statement and identify what could be done to improve next time. Remember that this should be a supportive space, so blaming individuals should be avoided. Instead, identify as a team how you can make adjustments and modifications. Allow a decent amount of time for this, so that a broad variety of ideas can be discussed and solutions identified.

When you've debriefed as a local team, if there were actions taking place in other locations make sure to debrief on a larger scale, following a similar process. Everyone who is interested should join the meeting and try to contribute to the conversation. Begin with an organiser from each team giving an explanation of how their action went, and the findings from their local debrief as to what went well and what didn't. You can then begin to identify parallels with successes and challenges between locations, and explore particular issues in further depth.

A useful technique is to approach this as a 'popcorn' brainstorm: if someone has a reflection or thought, it's immediately written down without question or critique. Then, when all ideas have been noted, they are all critically analysed. This allows for a great diversity of ideas and thoughts to be presented, with people not worrying about what they are proposing.

Step 25: What next? Building on momentum

Take time as a team to celebrate your achievements; although others may not recognise it, you all know just how much work went in to pulling this off. Once you've taken a bit of a rest, it's time to look at next steps. Often it's tempting to just re-do what's already worked; it's only logical to assume that recreating previous success is most effective. And, while this can work in the short term, it will generally lead to people becoming bored and disinterested in what you're doing. This is a scary thought to be confronted with; however, everyone at some point must overcome it. The key to having a network and audience that sticks around and continues to support the movement over time lies in using a variety of tactics. This particularly resonates during the COVID-19 crisis, a time when organisers across the world had to put current plans on hold and find new and creative forms of activism and protest to continue making change. All previous tactics had to be thrown out the window, to be replaced by various forms of online actions, and protests that an individual could take part in by themselves.

It's also vital to be constantly upskilling and training those who join the movement, so that as a group you have a continuous structure of new leaders and organisers keen to get involved and make effective change in their own communities. Take time to create internal systems of mentors who are able to teach and aid new volunteers; when working as *organisers* these systems are crucial. It can be a useful task to create training resources that can be distributed to new volunteers; in particular, resources that allow for a quick transition into the culture and systems implemented within your group. Additionally, for all leaders within the movement, frequent upskilling and training sessions from experienced activists and mentors are always invaluable.

A good way to ensure that your group stays strong through an extended period is to set up various action groups. These might be within schools, suburbs, electorates or cities, but they will all be autonomously organised groups falling under the same umbrella movement. In order for these action groups to work well and be effective, it's necessary for there to be a genuine community-driven interest in forming and acting as part of the group, rather than this being forced upon a location. As the umbrella movement, it's necessary to provide training, resources and other forms of support to these groups; however, this doesn't mean that action groups 'rank lower' or are of lesser importance than the more centralised part of the movement. In order for them to have the greatest local impact, you should seek to provide them with the skills they need to act independently to make change. If this doesn't happen, and strategy and tactical decisions aren't allowed to be made autonomously, it's likely that people won't feel much of a drive to take action and will feel disconnected from their community and the change they're aiming to make happen.

Eventually, hopefully, you will end up winning at least part of the battle you are fighting. Whenever this occurs make sure to send out the message of the people-power that has happened and to celebrate the win as much as you can.

MAJOR WINS ARE RARE IN ACTIVISM – BY VIRTUE OF THE SHEER SCALE OF THE ISSUES BEING FOUGHT – MEANING THEY SHOULD BE GREAT CAUSE FOR EXCITEMENT AND CELEBRATION.

However, it is unlikely that the entire issue has disappeared. Instead, you'll need to use the momentum that has brought you to this point and motivate it to move you on to the next struggle. Make a clear plan on how this will occur, but, most importantly, ensure you're still able to connect with your base. Find ways to frame this next issue in a similar way to the one you just beat, in order to show the urgency and need for action. Ideally, this should link back to your original demands, so that the messaging and overall ideology of the group is clear.

PART THREE

Powering your movement

For a movement to be successful, many things need to be running in conjunction. This can be overwhelming to navigate, as every group will have different methods that work for them. But what unifies all successful teams is quality communication on every level, both internally and externally. Communication is the lifeblood of any movement; the determiner of its success or failure. Without developed communication systems, everything has to be understood through a filter, which prevents you ever getting a clear image.

To keep a movement healthy, it's also vital for activists to look after themselves. Whether you're constantly involved, or occasionally throw yourself into the ring for one or two events that particularly resonate with you, stress and burnout are inevitable without proper self-care. It's hard, because slowing down and prioritising yourself can seem like the antithesis of the selfless nature of change-making. But being able to shape your activism to your own capacity is necessary if you want your involvement to be a healthy and positive experience, and your future activity to be sustainable and long lasting.

CHAPTER 6

PROMOTION – THE ART OF REACHING PEOPLE

FOR THE GROWTH AND DEVELOPMENT OF MOVEMENTS, AND the success of any action, promotion is key. In promoting your concept, you need to understand your 'target market' and, from there, find avenues to reach them. In addition to traditional media (newspapers, TV and so on), on-the-ground forms of communication can be very effective.

For a lot of events, you will have a specific market you want to 'target'. Often this will be a particular age group, profession, gender, sexual orientation, or such. As well as general promotion aimed at everybody, have materials and techniques that are specific to this group. You could approach local clubs and groups about promoting your project to their members through their email list or at their next meeting, ask community action groups for an endorsement or if you can arrange a speaking appearance at one of their meetings, and connect with online communities with a similar demographic to get a mention in a post or a shout out. To reach young people, ensure you're using digital methods, and try school clubs and sports teams, and create material they can share themselves. In essence, find spaces in which your 'target audience' are active and notice ways to reach them.

Creating resources and material that target these people will help you engage specifically with them. For example, for School Strike 4 Climate's first ever 'general strike' – when we were encouraging people from all walks of life to join – we created digital pamphlets on how to promote the strike within the workplace, and workers' rights surrounding it. Often you won't be able to receive an official endorsement of promotion from groups, particularly schools and workplaces; however, they are definitely still reachable. One great way to make contact is to thoroughly poster or hand out flyers outside these spaces. For example, in the lead-up to the March 15 school strike, we were aiming to reach school students. So, a friend and I caught a train and got off at every station that was near a school. We postered almost all the entrances to the school, all nearby bus stops and outside the train station. Along with the posters, we wrote chalk messages on the pavements:

Not only did this make sure a broad range of school students heard about the strike, but it removed a large amount of the feeling of alienation that people can have about attending.

One of the main goals of promotion is letting people know they won't be alone. It made students who were considering going – but were nervous that they might be the only one – feel safe that many others were talking about it and were likely to come along.

We also created school 'sign-up sheets', which a student would print out and then get those who were planning on attending to write down their names and contact information. Again, this helped students to know they weren't alone and, in turn, ensured that a large number of people would take part.

Posters and flyers

Posters and flyers are some of the simplest forms of outreach. Platforms such as Canva and Adobe Illustrator are useful for designing these. All information should be as clear as possible, and the design and fonts super eye-catching. If you have actions taking place in multiple cities, create a separate poster for each location, along with a blank version.

Make sure you have a high-quality version of your poster available online so that people can print it out for themselves and share it.

Postering is not only a cheap and effective means of promotion, it's also a fun activity that volunteers with any level of experience can take part in. Often groups will hold mass postering events (called a 'paint the town'), where a mass of people will meet in a central place to collect resources and then divide into smaller groups of two or three to target different locations. When you all meet together, it can be helpful to have a host assign areas for each group and talk through general advice. Explain which areas in particular should be targeted (such as main streets, train stations, schools and universities) and where should be avoided (any private property without asking for explicit permission). You can poster inside restaurants, shop windows and other businesses by asking permission. Make sure to provide plenty of wide clear tape, scissors (somehow nobody ever remembers these – you might become surprisingly proficient at tearing tape with your teeth), staple guns and different sizes of posters.

Depending on the number of volunteers and the size of the event you're promoting, you'll need to print anywhere between a couple of hundred and a few thousand posters. For most people, this isn't logistically possible using a home printer, and can be costly if you're paying for a printing service. Sometimes you'll be offered pro-bono printing services, so do reach out to print shops, NGOs, local politicians or workplaces that are supportive of your cause.

When you're handing out flyers, try to talk to people and spark up as much conversation as possible. When I was just starting to plan the first school strike in Sydney, I reached out to my local #StopAdani and GetUp groups for a space at their table at a local festival. They were very keen and supportive, which I really appreciated. While figuring out the logistics of the festival, I quickly learnt the event had a rule that you couldn't hand out flyers to everyone walking past, but were only able to offer them to people who were already interested. While this was great in theory, and eliminated buckets of paper waste from the event, I had to face the reality that I had to speak to countless strangers! I had printed off about 150 flyers the day before and so I got to work. Every time I saw a teenager, I would walk up to them before they passed me, and try to quickly say, 'Hey, there's a school strike for climate happening in a few weeks. I thought you might be interested.' While a lot ignored me, those who stopped to chat became interested and many pretty much guaranteed they would come along. By the end of the day I had handed out all the flyers and increased our potential turnout by quite a lot.

> **THE MOST EFFECTIVE FORMS OF PROMOTION WILL ALWAYS BE THOSE WHEN YOU THINK OUTSIDE THE BOX AND USE CREATIVE METHODS.**

People are used to seeing posters, flyers, emails and social media posts all over the place these days; however, if you're able to break through that and find a unique way to put yourself out there, you'll be significantly more noticeable and effective. Take time to look through what other movements have done and been successful with, and draw inspiration from what you think is most impactful and interesting.

The sky really is the limit when it comes to these techniques.

CHAPTER 7

HOW TO WRITE GREAT EMAILS

WHEN WRITING ANY EMAIL, IT'S IMPORTANT TO UNDERSTAND how formal or casual it needs to be. If you're addressing someone you work closely with and are on good terms with, formal structure and a professional tone are not of concern. In contrast, if you're getting in touch with someone you don't know particularly well or are just initiating contact with, you'll need to approach them in a more considered and formal manner.

Usually, it's best to begin your email by greeting the person with 'Hello <insert name>'. If you're emailing a general address or movement, you might want to open with 'To whom it may concern'. Depending on the broader tone of the email, it's often good to start with a pleasantry along the lines of 'I hope you've been well', then continue with 'I am writing to inform you...' If you've not been in touch with the person before, briefly explain who you are and what you do before introducing the important content. Outline why you are in contact: either what you're asking of them, or informing them of.

To conclude, as my mother advises: 'If you're over forty, sign off with "kind regards"; if you're a young person, just say "thanks".' Before pressing send, make sure to write a subject line that gives a brief overview of the email.

Create an email signature

An email signature is a bit of text that automatically adds itself to the end of every email you send. Typically it will feature your name, role within a group, contact information and sometimes an image or logo. Some people also include an Acknowledgement of Country and/or a message about considering the environment before printing. Here's what my email signature currently looks like:

Jean Hinchliffe
Organiser, School Strike 4 Climate
Mobile: +1234567890
IG: @jeanlola.h
Twitter: @jean_hinchliffe

I meet and work on the land of the Gadigal people of the Eora Nation. I pay respect to their Elders, past and present, and acknowledge the

> *pivotal role that Aboriginal and Torres Strait Islander people continue to play within the Australian community.*

I added a hyperlink so that when anyone clicks on 'School Strike 4 Climate' it directs them straight to our website.

Not only does a signature make your email look more professional, it makes sure that if someone has issues reaching you by email, they have an alternative way to get in touch.

CHAPTER 8

SOCIAL MEDIA – MAKE IT WORK FOR YOU

TO BE FRANK, I'M NOT GREAT ON SOCIAL MEDIA. ANYONE who follows my personal accounts would see my habit of posting a few times over one week, and then entirely neglecting the platform for the next couple months. In fact, I'm pretty awful when it comes to using technology in general, and I had to make far too many calls to friends to translate technical jargon I didn't understand when I was researching for this book. However ... social media is an extraordinarily useful tool in the activist world and definitely shouldn't be neglected. Not only is it a great place to spread the word about events and campaigns, it's also an amazing tool for educating a base.

Often when approaching the administration of a movement's social media accounts the amount of help required is underestimated. It's best to have a team of people who can divide up all the roles. Depending on the size of your team, you'll need different numbers of people in each role, with many probably taking on multiple roles, but a social media team might look something like this—

Regular posters: Every person has a pre-assigned day to post on social media each week. This ensures that every platform has consistent posting and the job is spread around.

Inbox admin: To go through all email requests and answer queries to the best of their ability, then put people in touch with the relevant organisers.

Story posters (for platforms, such as Instagram, with this feature): To share updates, current news, and anything that better suits the story format rather than a regular post.

Commenters: These people go through and 'like' all positive comments and respond to a large amount, as well as answering any questions. While they might need to occasionally respond to a slightly negative comment by clarifying facts, they shouldn't ever engage in arguments.

Designers: To create 'shareables' for social media. These might be posts with information about a particular topic, announcements, details for events, and so on. The main point is that they look eye-catching and appealing and are easy to understand and share.

You could have an Instagram account with tens of thousands of followers promoting an event, but it doesn't guarantee the event will get a high turnout. Large accounts typically feel disconnected and somewhat alien to the average person. However, when someone sees a whole group of their friends reposting the same promo material, or discussing a campaign they're interested in, or an event they're planning to go to, it feels much more personal – and much more important within their own community.

I remember when I announced on my personal Instagram story that the first Sydney School Strike 4 Climate was happening and that I was helping to organise it. I assumed it would be something that only my school friends, and potentially a few friends at different schools, would see. But that wasn't the case. Within 10 minutes or so a couple of people had screenshotted it and reposted it on their own pages, including someone who went to a different school from mine. Quite a few students at that school started sharing it, and it continued to spread further and further. Because people knew it was something of interest within their communities, they were much more inclined to commit to going and to continue spreading the word. This digital grassroots style of promotion was incredibly effective.

When you create social media posts, be sure you are making content that is easy to screenshot and share. Create posts that clearly state the purpose of your actions and provide specific event information and details that can be seen in just one image. It's also helpful to create content that people can get involved with – perhaps a particular hashtag, image type, and so on, which enables people to feel a deeper sense of engagement. Experiment with what content does and doesn't perform well on each platform; continue adjusting your approach based on what your audience enjoys and interacts with most.

It's also important to establish consistent procedures for posting on social media. This is less about the style of the content itself, and more so regarding the actual logistics of sharing it. If you're reposting anything, try to receive permission from the creator when possible, and always ensure credit is given clearly. Make your page accessible – caption videos, provide image descriptions through alt text, use easy to read fonts, avoid poorly contrasting colours and flashing or videos, and provide appropriate content warnings.

As your team grows, it's helpful to have a set list of social media guidelines. Make sure that anyone given access to passwords for accounts agrees to these terms, and that they're willing to hold themselves accountable. The guidelines might cover what sort of content can be posted and what shouldn't be, and when to block versus when to simply ignore people.

CHAPTER 9

THE POWER OF MAINSTREAM MEDIA

THE MAINSTREAM MEDIA (NATIONAL AND LOCAL NEWSPAPERS, TV, radio) is one of the most effective forms of communication you will use. Harness it to ensure people know about your movement, your actions and why you're doing what you're doing.

> **THE PHRASE 'THERE'S NO SUCH THING AS BAD PUBLICITY' TURNED OUT TO BE VERY APPROPRIATE FOR SCHOOL STRIKE 4 CLIMATE.**

Planning the first school strike was difficult in terms of reaching out to the public. As we were such a new group, we weren't taken seriously, and had difficulty getting in to the mainstream media cycle. If you talked to the average teenager even just a week before the strike, very few would have heard of us, and even fewer were planning on attending. That is, until our Prime Minister, Scott Morrison, responded to a question about us in Federal

Parliament. He was asked by Greens MP Adam Bandt whether he would 'listen to these kids, who are demanding action from your government to keep coal in the ground'. Morrison immediately expressed his dislike of 'kids not going to school' and infamously continued with: 'What we want is more learning in schools and less activism in schools.'

What I absolutely love about this story is that it was those comments that launched the Australian school strikes into the spotlight. The day after he made his response, I was suddenly put in contact with an enormous group of local and international media sources: people couldn't believe how tone-deaf the PM was, and they were eager to hear our side of the story. Despite this being just a few short days before the strike, the new-found media attention increased our potential turnout enormously.

> **HEARING A POLITICAL LEADER DELIVER SUCH CONDESCENDING COMMENTS MADE A LOT OF YOUNG PEOPLE VERY ANGRY; KNOWING HE WANTED TO QUASH OUR VOICES ONLY MADE US MORE MOTIVATED AND EAGER TO ACT.**

It also prompted some iconic protest signs, such as 'We'll be less activist if you'll be less shit'. Going into future events, gaining media traction was certainly a little easier. We were now well established and had proved we were able to motivate huge numbers of people to turn out. Suddenly, people from all walks of life began to view us as a serious social movement.

The press release

A press release is a statement that provides information about an event or story; it is sent out to journalists in the hope of having an article published about it. These press releases are vital if you want to get widespread media attention. They make the information and facts accessible, and, in many ways, they should look like your ideal news article. There are a few easy steps to follow in writing a killer press release to get your movement and event noticed.

- Start by formatting your release correctly. It should be able to be saved in a format such as PDF, doc or docx. Set your font size to 12 and leave a margin of at least 2 centimetres on each side. Write **Press Release** or **Media Alert** in bold at the top corner of the page. Underneath that, write the date that it will be sent out.

- Write a clear and catchy headline that gives a brief overview of the release and is less than 10 words long. This should read like any other news headline, such as 'Thousands attend student-organised environmental march'.
- In the first sentence of the press release you need to cover the most important points: the who, what, when, where and why of the situation.
- This is followed by the body of the piece, which explains everything in greater depth and provides compelling and interesting facts and statistics (make sure to supply sources when relevant). As you write, keep in mind that journalists often just skim-read press releases, so your information should be concise, clear and interesting.
- Include around three quotes from organisers or other significant people. These quotes should help show the broader context and importance of your story while also giving it a more intimate and personalised perspective.
- The release should be no longer than one page – all information should be snappy to ensure you keep the journalists' interest.
- Finish with the contact details of a media liaison person or anybody who has capacity

to handle the influx of phone calls and emails that are bound to follow.
- When you've finished writing, ask someone who knows very little about the situation to read through the text to check it makes complete sense. For a press release to be most effective, someone with no background knowledge of the situation should be able to read it and completely understand the issue at hand. If the release is about an event, they should now know exactly what they need to do to attend.

Contacting the media

Now you've written your press release, you need to get it out into the world. It's a good idea to create a 'media registry' to help you reach local and national media. This is a list that documents all the contact information you have with different news sources so that the information can be easily found and utilised. As you continue working as a group and developing relationships with individual journalists, getting media attention becomes a simpler process. But before you form these personal relationships, you should still be able to get in touch with news companies.

To start, create a list of every news company you'd *like* to get in touch with. Now do some online research, looking up '<insert company name> news press release contact'. You can also find the contact details of many journalists and media sources in online registries. Once you've written your press release, send it out to all relevant contacts, avoiding any journalists who specialise in a completely separate area, for example. It's good to follow this up with a phone call within the next day or so, confirming that the release was received.

When you first start out, your best bet for publicity is likely to be a local newspaper, which can create a strong impact within the community. Then, as you grow and develop as a group, you're more likely to receive broader media coverage. Don't forget, when you're targeting a local newspaper, try to include specific details that are locally relevant.

Doing an interview

When given media attention, always attempt to control the message you're projecting. In a way, the media should be thought of as a tool you use to push you and your message out into the world.

As a pretty simple example, during the lead-up to all events, SS4C ensure our main demands are mentioned in every interview. Although we only started as a group not long before our first event, we made sure that what we stood for was clearly defined. As we've progressed as a movement, this has helped make sure that what we are fighting for is always foremost in our messaging and group story. Having this unanimity on a national level also helps in our promotion, aiding in creating a core set of messages that we're able to share. It's important for your group to have a number of predetermined spokespeople who are all comfortable thinking on their feet and are prepared beforehand on how to behave in an interview.

To ensure that everyone keen to be a media spokesperson feels thoroughly prepared, hold a couple of training sessions. You'll find adult supporters are often happy to help with this, although they aren't a necessity. Try running a practice interview, complete with a variety of questions ranging from your personal story and motivations, to the aim of your initiative, to more hard-hitting awkward questions that play devil's advocate. If you are doing this in person, make sure that these interviews are recorded – although watching them back might make you cringe, it's one of the best ways to improve your technique.

I'll admit, my first media interview was a terrifying experience. It was with the *Education Review* podcast, a very small media site discussing the latest news in the riveting world of Australian education. At the time of writing, there have been only 213 listeners to the interview; however, as I prepared I remember it feeling like one of the most high-pressure situations I had ever been in. I had scheduled the call for after school and as soon as I got home I checked that my phone was fully charged (and not secretly about to die on 2 per cent). I gave everyone in my family strict instructions that no one could come into the front room until I opened the door. I sat on the couch, constantly checking my phone to see if it had managed to turn itself to silent or miss an unfamiliar number. Finally, after what felt like hours, the call came through. I picked up and began running the standard course. 'Yes, this is Jean. Good, thanks; how are you? Of course you can record this.' At last the questions began. The journalist asked me about my inspirations, my role within the group, the importance of the strike, and so on. (Fun fact – it was during this interview that I labelled myself a 'lead organiser'. The term hadn't been used at all beforehand, but as I continued using it in other interviews it suddenly became a common phrase within the SS4C movement.) With each answer I gave, I physically cringed at how awful I thought I sounded. In my mind I had either phrased something completely wrong or didn't make any sense or just sounded like an idiot.

When the interview finally came to a close I tried my hardest to forget the whole experience, telling my school friends that it was dreadful and they couldn't listen. However, they were quick to Google and find the whole thing online, much to my disdain. This prompted a couple of my friends to make a remix of the interview; in particular, the moments I hated most. To this day I can barely listen to it without cringing, although I'll admit it was very funny of them.

How to talk ... and breathe!

Going into any interview, you should know what you want to portray and what needs to be said. I recommend always trying to include all your group's demands, any key messaging and a statistic or two that you can quote to prove your point. You should be able to quote all of these very easily when asked. However, it's important that your response doesn't sound overly scripted; it should feel natural and you should come across as though you're answering in the moment.

Depending on the structure of the interview, the audience may or may not hear the question. If not, you'll be asked to incorporate the question into your answer. You've probably had to do this a lot at school: it's known as 'answering in full sentences' (for example, 'My favourite colour is green', rather than just 'green'). If a question is difficult and you're not sure how to answer, try to link it back to your core messaging and demands and continue from there. Try to keep your answers brief and understandable: you want the information you're conveying to feel accessible to someone who doesn't know much about the topic. Make sure you're aware of what information can be considered assumed knowledge and what you need to explain; it's easy to forget that many people aren't well informed of your issue.

Often, when asked questions, you might feel as if you must respond immediately. This can lead to stumbling over words and rushing answers. If a question is difficult, or you're not 100 per cent sure how to answer, feel free to take a moment to gather your thoughts. Take a deep breath and slow yourself down a little, then, once you feel ready, go into answering.

It's easy to become tense when talking to the media; with all the nerves and pressure surrounding you, it's natural. Try to be aware of your physicality: drop your shoulders, unclench your jaw and relax your hands. As a typical film interview will be fairly close up, be careful not to move around too much or too fast; in particular, if you're sitting in a swivel chair (a personal struggle of mine!).

And, remember: if you're unhappy with how you responded to a question or if you accidentally stumbled over words or stated something incorrectly, you're allowed to retake your response. No one is perfect and, as most television interviews are pre-recorded, it's very easy to edit around anything. All you need to say is: 'I'm sorry, could I try that one again?'

Sharing the media spotlight

While opportunities for media interviews should be divided up as fairly as possible within your group, it's also important to prioritise marginalised voices, in particular those most impacted by the issue. When you exist in a society where those of less privilege are systematically oppressed and silenced, it's vital that you use your platform to help dismantle these issues. While the media might like the sight of a conventionally televisual white teenager, it doesn't mean you shouldn't be doing all you can to pass the microphone to those who are often left voiceless.

> **IT'S EASY TO BE RELIANT ON A FEW VOICES TO REFLECT THE MANY, BUT THAT WILL ONLY WEAKEN A MOVEMENT.**

Try to have spokespeople from diverse backgrounds and with different stories. You should have people from the inner city, from regional and rural areas, people who identify as LGBTQ+, people of colour, Indigenous folx, disabled and neurodiverse people, people from a variety of socio-economic backgrounds, and so on. If a new story relates particularly to one sort of issue, ensure that you have a spokesperson who has a personal connection with the problem. For example, if the media reaches out to your environmental group for a segment about bushfires, have a spokesperson who has been directly impacted so they can share their story.

You'll find that as you begin to receive more media attention that only a small portion of your team will consistently have their voices uplifted through disproportionate amounts of media attention. I know that I've been this person in the past, and while it feels nice and validating to receive credit for your work, it can distract from what is most important. If you notice yourself receiving more media than is fair, try to take a break from media for some time, or impose rules upon yourself, such as only taking every other opportunity offered, or only taking interviews from media that has contacted you directly rather than putting up your hand as a spokesperson. The goal is to ensure a diverse and accurate image of the movement is represented, and that you don't receive unfair levels of attention for what is everybody's work.

CHAPTER 10

PUBLIC SPEAKING

PUBLIC SPEAKING TENDS TO BE ONE OF THE MOST SCARY and difficult elements of activism for many people. The idea of speaking in front of a class of friends can be daunting, let alone speaking on a panel, at a function or to a crowd of hundreds or even thousands at a rally. However, with adequate preparation these nerves are completely conquerable.

Start by considering the context in which you will be speaking—
- What is the focus of the event?
- What demographic of people will be present?
- What message do you need to get across?
- How well informed will your audience be about your issue?

For example, if you're going to speak at a rally, assume the audience has a solid base of information but not all the specific details; whereas, if you were to present to a group of adult specialists, you might assume they fully understand the specifics of the issue. So, understand when knowledge should be assumed, but remember that it's always best to be more accessible.

The rally speech

A speech for a rally is completely different to one you would present at school, for example, in language and structure, and in delivery. Begin by introducing yourself, including your name, the group you work with and potentially your age and grade at school. Then I like to give a brief overview of my experience as an activist within that space. For example: 'Hi, I'm Jean. I'm a climate striker and sixteen-year-old student at Fort Street High School. I founded the Sydney group of School Strike 4 Climate in October 2018 and have been working nonstop since then to achieve climate justice.'

Speaking at a rally is quite a surreal experience. In a weird way, I find it easier to speak to thousands of people than I do to my English class. On 20 September 2019, 80,000 people poured into the Domain in Sydney – this remains the largest rally I've ever spoken at. Fellow striker Daisy Jeffrey and I were MCs at the event, which was an incredible privilege. The entire time I was speaking, I was thinking how I simply couldn't comprehend a crowd that big. It was so vast and chaotic and amazing that my brain just wouldn't process it. Every line I said was followed by an overwhelming cheer from the crowd; the energy was simply electric. Despite the heat, the sound system not being the size it needed to be, and the amount of people crammed into the space, it seemed that they were only growing more energetic as time went on.

> **KNOWING YOU'RE IN A SPACE WITH TENS OF THOUSANDS OF PEOPLE WHO ARE JUST AS ANGRY AS YOU ARE IS A SPECIAL FEELING, AND BEING AT THE FRONT OF IT ALL IS A TRULY UNFORGETTABLE EXPERIENCE.**

When you're preparing to speak at a rally, remember that those in attendance are already on your side. Your speech isn't to convince them that what you are saying is something they should care about; instead, you're aiming to tell a story and explain the situation and shortcomings of those who should be solving this problem. Think about how it impacts you in a personal sense, and how you can explain the cause in an engaging and passionate way. Additionally, include relevant statistics and facts that will further your point, particularly when they're paired with emotive and passionate language. Ensure the goals of your movement are stated at the beginning and end of the speech. You should also make sure to have a few 'show-stopping' lines – the moments where your point is drilled home with an impactful and memorable statement. Here are some pointers for a great rally speech—

- Projection is hugely important for you to be heard and sound confident. To project your voice, you need to breathe deeply in order to expand your diaphragm. It's an odd feeling, as if you're breathing into the very bottom of your stomach instead of your lungs.
- As you speak, make sure to articulate every word and attempt to sound 'larger' rather than 'louder'. That means that instead of just trying to yell, you extend your mouth and throat.
- Take a moment to breathe between lines so that you can continue speaking, and also pause to allow more important lines to sink in.
- Speak very clearly, loudly and confidently. It's an emotional way of speaking: you're spending your time trying to make people even more passionate and invigorated than they already are. So be emotive in your delivery; allow your anger, dismay, hope,

love, or whatever else you're feeling, to shine through.
- When you reach one of your 'show-stopping' lines, make sure you put extra emphasis on it, and allow time for cheering and applause afterwards.

- If people cheer or make a noise in a spot you weren't expecting, be sure to pause for a few seconds before you continue with your next line. And always repeat or start a line again if people weren't able to hear you because of noise.
- If you feel nervous just before you speak, take a moment to have a sip of water, and breathe deeply and slowly in and out for a

minute. In the moment, remind yourself that you deserve to be there, your voice is important and what you have to say really does matter.
- Ultimately, the best aid to a smooth performance is knowing your speech inside and out.

Speaking at a more formal and less energetic event is, of course, considerably different. Remember to speak clearly and continue projecting; however, the whole speech will be vastly less 'yell-y'. Most often you will be there to inform and persuade, and the subject matter will need to be adjusted to match. Rather than attempting to stir up the crowd, your goal is now to convince somebody of your argument. So your language might be more complex and your argument presented in far more depth than at a rally. This sort of speech is often more reliant on providing evidence than searching for an emotive response, but at the end of the day it will use both.

Panel speaking

Speaking on a panel is a fun form of public speaking. You typically go into it not knowing any of the questions that will be asked, so it relies on your being able to think on your feet and answer questions well in a short amount of time. If you're asked to speak on a panel and you don't already know everybody else speaking, learn their names, faces and what they do before you arrive. It can come off as disrespectful to turn up and not know anything whatsoever about the other panel members.

When a question is asked, it can sometimes feel a little awkward working out who will answer it if it hasn't been directed at any one panel member, but this isn't a major issue. If a question is given to someone else but you'd like to answer it, as the person speaking ahead of you finishes, simply reach for the mic and mention that you'd also like to answer. However, try not to do this too frequently: moderators will typically try to distribute questions as equally as possible, to ensure a balanced conversation that doesn't run over time.

Networking

One thing about being asked to speak at events is that you get to meet all kinds of interesting people. Networking seems like such a scary term, giving off an aura of tech start-ups and middle-aged people in business suits. However, it's a simple and often really fun activity. In essence, networking is making new relationships with people who share a common interest or work in a similar sector to your own.

It's a useful tool in activism: you never know who might end up being a vital contact for a campaign. While networking is not generally what we think of as 'public speaking', gaining the confidence to talk to new people and make new connections is a genuine skill that takes practice.

In late September 2019, I was in New York for Climate Week. It was an insane period, and I spent my whole time darting between events and meetings and more events. I quickly found a group of people to hang out with, which included a climate activist and now great friend of mine, Jonah Gottlieb. He was nicknamed 'the politician' in our circle, in part because of his very 'politician-esque' sense of style, but mostly due to his incredibly impressive, albeit hilarious, networking skills. No matter the event, he would spot someone he knew he wanted to speak to. He'd dash over in a most distinctive manner, leaning forwards at a harsh angle while leading with his head; it was as if his brain was urgently pulling him somewhere before his body could react. This was always followed with a confident handshake and an instant break into lengthy conversation.

One evening, a group of us went to an event about the ways in which Indigenous Amazonian people use activism to protect the Amazon rainforest. That same night it was our friend Kevin's birthday dinner, which was set to start about half an hour before the event finished. We concluded that, if we timed it well, we would just be able to make it to his dinner before we became undeniably, unfashionably late. Unfortunately, as we were ready to get going, we realised Jonah – who was dressed in a new purple blazer that only elevated his 'politician' status – was missing; he was deep in conversation with a group of speakers from the event. Of course, we didn't want to interrupt, so we waited as he continued chatting for a further 5, 10, 15 minutes, conjuring up more and more to discuss. He finally came back to our group and we made a mad dash to an Uber, which (of course) got stuck in traffic. The waiter gave us an annoyed look as at last we took our seats in the near empty restaurant, ready to down absurd volumes of authentic Italian carbs. We had a time limit of less than an hour to get out of there before it closed for the evening, resulting in a collective speed-run of pizza and soft drink consumption. Although we did arrive deeply late, I don't think it was in vain – Jonah had undoubtedly enjoyed some excellent networking time and made new relationships that would come into good use in the future.

Before you attend any speaking event, summit, panel, or the like, see if you can find a list of people who might be in attendance or who are officially involved to discover if there's anyone you're keen to meet.

I know there have been several occasions when I was in the same space as someone I had already heard of and found impressive, yet I missed meeting them due to a lack of research paired with my incredibly poor facial recognition skills. Realising later that this has happened is probably one of the most frustrating feelings imaginable.

If there's someone you want to speak to, when you can see they've reached the end of a conversation or are alone for a few moments, step in and introduce yourself. This might feel a little awkward or uncomfortable the first few times you do it, but the more you try, the more natural and relaxed you will become. Try to appear confident by making eye contact and smiling, then explain very briefly who you are and what you do. Ask questions and try to enjoy the experience as a conversation rather than a way to find another person who might help you out. There are no strict guidelines for what you should talk about – just say whatever feels natural establish a genuine connection with the person. Make sure to exchange contact information; store this in a safe place and add it to your contacts as soon as possible. In the next week or so, follow up with an email or text to everyone you met, explaining how it was great to talk to them and how keen you are to stay in touch.

Even if you're unsure of who the people around you are, initiating conversation is always worthwhile. I can't tell you how many times someone I met briefly, then followed on Instagram, ended up being helpful in providing an element that pulled together a whole event. And, not only is it useful, but getting to know other people who are similarly passionate about social issues is a truly enjoyable experience.

If you see someone standing alone at an event, instead of just making awkward eye contact and then pretending you never saw each other, approach them and introduce yourself. It can be nerve-wracking when it's a complete stranger, but the connections made will totally outweigh the initial awkwardness.

CHAPTER 11

COMMUNICATION WITHIN THE TEAM

WHILE TEXTING IN SOCIAL MEDIA GROUP CHATS OR MEETING during lunch at school initially works fine for keeping in touch, as your team grows you'll quickly learn the need for formal methods of communication. To work best together, everyone needs to know what's going on so no one is left out. Otherwise, you'll be plagued by constant miscommunication, leading to disorganisation and unnecessary discord within your team. This might feel like an easy thing to sort out, but taking the time to find what works best for your group will greatly elevate your activism.

Slack and other chats

Here, I must bring up a deep, dark period in School Strike 4 Climate history, a period defined by chaos and anarchy, and a moment every organiser seeks to forget — the eight months when our entire network communicated almost exclusively by Facebook Messenger. During the summer of 2018–19, the national SS4C group set up a Slack workspace – a server-like communication platform primarily used by businesses. However, as most local SS4C groups were still very small, many were using alternative platforms, such as WhatsApp or Facebook Messenger. This system worked quite well, and gave local groups an amount of autonomy in how they organised. Despite organising nationally on Slack, we decided to make one group chat, called the 'Student Support Network', on Messenger. This would be for when advice was needed very quickly; however, not in a binding or official way.

The system worked well for a while. Messenger was a friendly, relaxed space that everybody loved because it was much easier to navigate than Slack. Soon enough, more and more important conversations were being conducted over this support network. Slowly, but inexorably, it transformed into our main organising space, which became incredibly hard to follow. Having over a hundred people on one chat, with a good portion of them being very active, quickly translated into an overflow of messages with no chance of ever catching up on them. Eventually, other chats popped up for different working groups and particular tasks, all of which required a specific link or digital invite to join. This continued happening over the course of the year, to the point where there were easily 100 different chats that we somehow needed to be on top of, although most people were in only a small fraction of them. It was complete and utter chaos. If I turned my notifications on for even just one minute, I would be bombarded with message after message, most of which weren't important or relevant to me. On top of this, being in chats where everyone is constantly emoji-reacting to others and responding at rapid-fire pace is insanely stressful. I felt if I looked away from it for a moment everything would fall apart and I'd have no clue what was going on.

For months I compulsively checked my phone all the time to see everything I'd missed, and tried to weigh in on debates and decision-making the moment they were happening. It became a breeding ground for tense conversation and arguments, as everyone was involved in the dialogue, or was at least watching and reacting to messages in real time. It was occasionally brought up that we should revert back to Slack and, in all honesty, I was originally against this proposal. While Messenger was stressful as hell, at least it all made sense. To me, Slack seemed the epitome of boomer technology: functionally fine, but impossible to navigate. However, a thorough analysis of seemingly every messaging app on the internet revealed what should've been obvious to us all along: our system was awful. Completely and utterly unusable, some might suggest. So we began the treacherous process of reaching a network-wide agreement that we needed something different and, once we reached that consensus, we somehow had to get everybody to change platforms again. It took call after poll after call until, at last, we made the choice official. At long last, the transition came. The tech team killed every chat, one by one, occasionally accompanied with a gif of Moe from *The Simpsons* throwing people out of a bar, captioned 'PURGE TIME'.

Don't make the same mistakes we did.

Once you have a team working together, having a conversation platform is super important. If you have a small group working closely, a group chat on something like Facebook Messenger or an Instagram group chat can work really well. However, as your team grows, you'll need to transfer to a more functional and customisable platform.

Apps such as Slack and Discord allow you to create a server with different chats, which can be private or open for everyone to join. On Discord, whenever someone joins they will automatically be able to access and immediately see all chats, other than those set to 'private', whereas on Slack they can look through and pick which conversations are relevant to them that they want to join. If you need something more confidential, I've found Telegram works well, though can grow tricky to navigate as more and more separate chats are created.

There's a plethora of options out there for group communication. Some will cost money depending on the amount of users, while others are entirely free and accessible. Some will be suited to a team of hundreds, while others might be more effective for small numbers. Spend time researching which are best suited to your needs.

When chats go wrong

Group chat spaces can sometimes grow tense, even toxic, due to the constant activity and lack of clarity of tone in texted messages as opposed to face-to-face meetings. Writing a set of rules early on – an etiquette – for everyone to follow, can help prevent this. They might look like this –

- This is a work space, so keep all conversation relevant. If you want to chat or talk about off-topic issues, transfer to a different space.
- Respect others – there should never be abusive or offensive language.

- Keep the conversation constructive. Don't discredit or trash another person's ideas or thoughts. It could prevent them feeling comfortable sharing ideas in the future.
- Remember the difference between a conversation and an argument: a conversation is when you are trying to reach a conclusion together; an argument is trying to prove who is right.
- If everyone is in a similar time zone, it can be helpful to have a curfew of sorts for ending conversations so that you don't stay up all night talking.
- If something can't be resolved through messaging, pause until there is a suitable time to have a call or discussion.

If communication *does* become difficult, it can be useful to develop a mediation team. This is a group of people who facilitate conversation and help resolve disagreements or inappropriate behaviour.

It can take trial and error to determine what works best for you as a group, so don't be afraid to change how it operates if things aren't working.

Ensure that anyone involved in facilitating the mediation process remains neutral, and holds themself accountable to do so. If people feel they're being treated unfairly, it's vital that a system is created for them to explain their problem with the process and for action to be taken.

Mediation can take place in a variety of different ways. Sometimes just having a call with a neutral facilitator is all that's needed to sort things out; at other times, consequences might be needed in response to inappropriate behaviour. Consequences of any sort should always be a last resort: you don't want people to feel scared of honesty or concerned that it's too easy to have measures taken against them. Additionally, pettiness can develop in private relationships and cause difficulties that far exceed what is reasonable. Again, it is the role of mediators to call out this behaviour and take time to explain the importance of keeping 'private' relationships out of activism spaces. The aim is to ensure that the team feels comfortable working together and that internal issues don't take away from what's most important.

Online meetings

In my opinion, an in-person meeting is always preferable to meeting online. Obviously, this isn't possible in all situations. Even for teams who are situated in the same city it can be a major challenge – at the time of writing, the Sydney

SS4C team has only ever had a handful of in-person meetings. So, if you can't meet up physically, the best substitute is generally video calling.

You can video call through social media (Instagram and Facebook both have options), or use a service designed specifically for online meetings. Platforms such as Zoom, Google Meet, BlueJeans, Skype, Microsoft Teams and so on have a bunch of useful tools, depending on your requirements. For most of these platforms you'll get a unique link for each call, making it easy for everyone to gain access to it. Additionally, some have the option to dial in from a phone, so that people with no internet access are able to join the meeting. Many also have the option of 'breakout rooms', so you can separate into small groups for discussion before coming back into the main space together. However, some platforms cost money to have a premium account, which might be a point of difficulty. Again, take time to research and decide what will work best for your team.

Before each call, make sure there's a set agenda so that conversation is relevant and productive. This agenda might sit anywhere on the scale of general and loose to hyper-structured, depending on the formality of the meeting and the number of people planning to attend. When the call is small and generally for brainstorming or doesn't have a strict time limit, you can get away with having a rough idea of what needs to be covered. When there are multiple important topics to get through, you'll need to have a more structured conversation, otherwise it's easy to drift off task. List the topics to be covered on the agenda, and note down who will introduce and explain each topic to the group.

It's also important to have a clear etiquette outlined for video calls. Depending on the size of the group, and the relationships within it, this will vary a bit. Typically, the guidelines might look like this –

- Keep your microphone on mute unless you're speaking.
- Keep what is said relevant to the topic.
- Wait your turn to speak, treat everyone with respect and listen to instruction from the facilitator.

It's also essential to have a minute-keeper to write notes about the meeting as it happens. These notes should preferably be written directly into the agenda document and don't need to be particularly in depth.

How to facilitate an online video meeting

The role of a meeting facilitator is key to ensuring that meetings run smoothly and that everyone has a chance to speak. After waiting about 5–10 minutes until everyone's organised and has joined, they will typically deliver an Acknowledgement of Country before starting on the meeting agenda. For each point on the agenda, they should introduce the topic and then refer to whoever has been assigned to explain it further. When the participants have queries or responses to this, it's important for them to indicate that to the facilitator.

Having a predetermined group of symbols in the chat box (if that's a function on the platform you're using) helps a bunch. For example, sending * on a chat is the equivalent of putting your hand up, and shows you want to speak – this allows the facilitator to keep track of who has spoken and who will go next. Some platforms allow for a 'hands up' feature, although this can be hard to navigate and might not show the order in which questions were asked. The symbols ^ and + are also commonly used to show that you either agree with the message above or agree with what someone is saying while they're speaking. This makes it easy to see general support for something without having too much clutter or confusion.

School Strike 4 Climate have come up with a system to send * in the chat when a general point is being made, as the equivalent of putting your hand up, and @ when someone wants to directly respond to a point. Seeing these, the facilitator will then 'pass the mic' to each person wanting to speak, prioritising direct responses first, and then moving through the * signs. It's also helpful at this stage for the facilitator to read aloud any messages expressing opinions that were sent in the chat, so that anyone who missed them can hear the point.

Throughout the meeting, the facilitator should ask relevant questions and help guide a productive conversation. They should also be wary of participants who are speaking more than others, and ask for the opinions of those who've been quieter throughout the call. Additionally, they should ensure that conversation doesn't stretch on too long so that the meeting finishes at a reasonable time.

If a quick decision needs to be made, relevant only to that meeting, such as whether you should continue discussing a particular point, the facilitator could conduct a quick 'temp check' to figure out everyone's opinion. This means asking a yes or no question, then asking everyone to place their hands up (as if they were going to give a high five) if they agree, fingers flat if they're neutral, or fingers down if they're in opposition. However, if a more official decision needs to be made, it's helpful to have a better method of voting. This might involve sending Yes, No or Abstain to the chatbox, filling out an online form, or using a polling function of the call platform.

CHAPTER 12

TIME MANAGEMENT

TRYING TO BALANCE ACTIVISM WITH SCHOOL AND OTHER extra-curricular activities is a massive task. Not only does activism take up a large chunk of time, but unfortunately you can't opt out of assignments and homework in order to make more space for it! In complete honesty, I'm terrible at managing my time. Since primary school I've been a chronic procrastinator, who then gets enormously anxious the moment there are any consequences to my actions or, more specifically, lack of action. However, I've found several strategies that help make it a little bit easier to balance everything.

My number one strategy is to not just *buy* a pretty calendar or diary, but to actually *use* it.

Every time you're given an assignment, date for a test, meeting time, party invite, or deadline of any kind, NOTE IT DOWN.

Don't wait until later in the day, or assume you'll be able to remember everything – trust me, you won't. I find a digital calendar works best for me – I'm able to sync it with my phone so that a notification pops up 30 minutes before any meeting begins, and a reminder appears a few days before any important schoolwork is due. Some people might prefer a physical diary though: they're practical and easy to look through and jot down notes at any point. Despite this, neither of these will work unless you develop a strong habit of writing down all important information as soon as it comes to you.

It's also useful to create a schedule every week.

Part of being an activist is that you'll have an irregular and ever-changing schedule, so it's hard to have a plan that works all of the time.

However, it's always worth spending 15 minutes at the beginning of every week to make a plan for what needs doing on which day, taking into consideration all the blocks of time you've already dedicated to different meetings and calls. Don't only schedule in time for work; make time to have a social life and hang out with friends, and to chill and reset too. This is necessary if you're going to stick to a schedule and still have a balanced lifestyle.

Make sure to let relevant people know when your life is going to get particularly hectic and busy. If you have exams coming up, let your fellow organisers know that you won't have much capacity at that time. Similarly, if you're in the lead-up to a major action or event, make sure your school and teachers are aware so that they can try to be understanding of your circumstances. While it can be easy to try to separate the two, or assume you'll be able to handle everything fine, this communication is important for keeping a healthy workload in each area.

You should also try to remember that you can't do everything, and your occasional absence will not be the end of the world. When you're so invested in a project or cause, it can be hard to take a step back and allow yourself to focus on other priorities. This sometimes manifests as being hyper-controlling of a team, or worrying that things will start to fall apart without your involvement. Remind yourself that everyone else involved has aptitude and is worthy of trust; they'll be able to continue getting good work done without your presence. Not feeling pressure to always be involved can lighten the load you feel, even if you end up completing the same amount of work.

Manage your email

I must say, I'm awful at remembering to reply to emails. I've often reached the point when I feel a deep sense of dread about even looking at my inbox, which only leads to putting it off further. For a while, my mum ended up being a temporary administrator for my email, as it became too much for me to handle. While this might seem ridiculous, it's been a genuine issue for me and many others (inbox anxiety is all too real!) and I can guarantee my long-suffering publisher has had to put up with this unfortunate trait of mine. Here are some quick email guidelines that might help –

- To keep your inbox tidy, in an ideal world you'd reply to emails soon after they arrive. If, however, you find yourself replying weeks after the initial contact, it's not the end of the world; remind yourself that any response is better than none.
- When your inbox is clogged up, take 5–10 minutes to go through it and flag those you haven't yet replied to. At this point, don't even worry about responding to anything; this is just about knowing exactly what needs to get done.
- Once all the unanswered emails are flagged, start replying to them. This is probably the most daunting part of the process, but you'll feel so refreshed and relieved afterwards. Remember to take it one step at a time.
- Some emails require a quick read, then you smile at the emoji and delete them.
- Remember that if someone is asking a favour of you, or requesting a speaking or

media engagement that you're too tired to do or are not that keen on, you're allowed to say no and pass it on to someone else!

Keep your inbox in order

For the many emails that relate to a project, or that you'll need to keep and refer back to, you have to create a whole bunch of labels and folders. Typically, this filing needs to be done on a desktop or laptop rather than a mobile device. Start off by making a few broad folders, encompassing whole projects or concepts (such as social media, national work and so on). When you're new to filing, these broader systems can work well for a while. However, it can be a big help to categorise them even further. Within these broader folders, create some more specific files – perhaps you have a broad 'Rally @ ScoMo's office' folder; within that you might have 'program planning', 'media' and 'police communications' folders. As time goes on, you'll end up with a whole array of these smaller folders and you might need to create new ones or merge some as a project develops. You need to commit to consistently using these folders, otherwise you'll have a whole heap that aren't up to date, which is why starting with a few big categories and progressing from there can be much more manageable.

Once you've tidied up your inbox, if you want to keep that lovely feeling of order, unsubscribe from any promotional material or newsletters you barely read or have no interest in. This means you'll only receive emails that are relevant or important to you, and makes decluttering in the future much simpler. (This seems obvious, but I know I rarely take the time to do it. I feel like this might be a uniquely 'meproblem', but I always feel bad deleting any emails at all – what if that conversation I forgot about from a year ago is suddenly relevant again tomorrow? – which means my inbox always has too much mail in it and searching for anything is total chaos. Just fight that impulse, and a happily uncluttered inbox will be yours.)

CHAPTER 13

LONGEVITY: TAKING CARE OF YOURSELF AND EACH OTHER

ALTHOUGH NOT UNEXPECTED, IT'S RIDICULOUS HOW undervalued self-care is, not just to activists, but to society in general. Instead, we resort to working ourselves far harder than is necessary, until it stops being enjoyable and fulfilling.

Self-care is just as important as any other element of activism. Not only does it help you stay within the movement for the long haul, it allows for your work to be more effective and impactful.

Personal self-care

The form of care that is most commonly talked about is personal self-care. This is typically portrayed as a deep bubble bath surrounded by scented candles, a cucumber face mask and a large helping of chocolate cake. And, don't get me wrong, these can certainly be helpful to your mood. However, I think this creates an unrealistic vision of what self-care can and should be, and also doesn't get to the root causes of why it might be needed. While a practical and tangible form of self-care is useful at times, recognising the unhealthy mindsets you might have, and working towards a healthier way of thinking, is equally – if not more – important, but often overlooked.

A mindset I've held for most of my life, and only recently been attempting to work through, is constantly comparing myself to others. Growing up, I was a dance-obsessed kid who dreamt of being a ballet dancer. I would watch YouTube videos of dance prodigies and panic about how much better than me they were, and then spend too much time convincing myself that if I just tried a little bit harder, and put in a little more work, in one year's time I'd be just as good. When I quit ballet and fell in love with acting, I watched shows starring kids the same age as me and, sure enough, I started to obsess about how they were all miles ahead of me. By the time I became involved in activism, I found it hard not to compare myself to the 'famous' activists in the US or the enormously experienced and eloquent activists I'd just started working with. When someone mentioned to me that those people I was always comparing myself to were probably doing the same towards me, I couldn't believe it at all.

This sort of mindset forces you to always believe that, no matter how hard you try, you'll never be enough. Part of what makes this mentally so toxic is that, in the age of social media, people are only sharing and promoting the exciting and positive moments in their lives. Nobody is broadcasting the days when they're incredibly unproductive, or things aren't going according to plan. Social media can warp the image of a person, making them seem impressive and unattainable. It takes a whole lot of work to change your way of thinking, but not doing so only causes harm. By growing jealous of others' opportunities and recognition, it places these attributes above what is most important – trying to make the world a better place. While that side of activism is exciting – and somewhat 'glamorous' – on-the-ground grassroots work, done as a caring and unified collective, will always be number one. Although it's hard to recognise, it's vital to realise that everyone is on their own journey, and someone else's successes and opportunities are in no way indicative of your failures. When you catch yourself growing jealous of others, or feeling you are 'lesser', take time to slow down and remind yourself that just because one person has an opportunity that you don't, it doesn't mean all the amazing work you've done suddenly isn't 'valid' or important. You are at one point in your journey, and that is perfectly okay.

If there are particular people you notice who make you feel this way, try muting them on social media or unfollowing them. If you feel it's become a major issue with somebody you work with and is inhibiting your relationship with them, or if they're behaving in a certain way around you that seems to be making the issue worse, try to reach out and have an honest dialogue about how you're feeling.

Burnout

Another mindset that most of us hold to some degree, is the idea that productivity is directly associated with your worth as a person. This culture of always needing to be active and making something 'of worth' is a byproduct of the market's dominating role in our public arena; it's come from the corporate world and is immensely pervasive in our day-to-day lives. It can be seen in the constant need to monetise and commodify our hobbies and interests; in the world of activism it creates a deep sense of guilt if you aren't always working. Since what we do can often feel like the most important thing in the world, it seems we're 'wasting time' or being 'bad' activists by not spending every waking moment on our work. When we're addressing such enormous issues, it can feel like nothing anyone does is ever enough. On top of this, it's common for people to feel an enormous sense of imposter syndrome, as if they don't deserve to be in the space, and that they need to prove themselves 'worthy' by pushing themselves unnecessarily hard. When you have this amount of pressure placed on you, it's only natural to work far beyond your healthy limit and, when you're pushing your body far beyond what it physically or mentally can tolerate, it inevitably translates to burnout.

Burnout is the point at which you've worked through all your mental and physical energy in an unsustainable way, causing a major collapse in motivation and your personal capacity to do the work you find important. Learning how to avoid burnout in the first place is vital; but, if it does ever happen, you should have the skills to be able to overcome it.

- Try to create boundaries between work and life. I, for one, am awful at this; however, implementing even subtle changes has helped me.
- Turn off phone notifications during school hours or after a certain time at night.

- If you're engaged with another activity or out with people, turn off your phone so that you don't feel tempted to reply to yet another 'important' message. Trust me, it can wait for a couple of hours.
- Allocate an afternoon, evening or day each week when you make time just for yourself. Maybe catch up with friends, practise a hobby, or take that hour-long bubble bath. This time is purely for you.
- If you *are* experiencing burnout, take a break. Step aside from activism for a weekend, or a fortnight, or a couple of months – however much time you feel you need to recover. When you feel you're in a better headspace, try gradually returning to these spaces. Maybe you'll only be active in one working group for a week or so, before adding more to your workload again, or maybe you'll just join one call each week or limit the amount of time you want to work. It's all about experimenting and finding the right balance for you.

Being able to understand your own capacity and limits, and to overcome burnout, are essential skills for an activist. This will ensure you're as effective and motivated in your work as possible.

A balance of interests

When you become completely immersed in your work, it's easy for it to dominate your life and become a core part of your identity. Rather than you being a piece in the movement, the movement becomes a piece of you, which is really unhealthy. This means that whenever an action doesn't go quite as well as planned, a piece of important legislation isn't passed, or an election doesn't go in your favour, rather than recognising it as a shortcoming within the movement, it becomes a personal failure. This not only places unnecessarily pressure on every step you take as a group, but it puts you in a position that isn't healthy or sustainable.

Ultimately, to live in the healthiest way, make sure your world encompasses far more than just your activism. In the same way that an ecosystem needs a great variety of life within it for it to thrive, to be a motivated and mentally healthy person you can't have a monoculture of interests and ways you spend your time. I've provided a couple of handy charts to help explain this concept.

If you look at the first chart, you can see that one pastime, let's say it's activism, totally dominates, leaving little room for other things, such as schoolwork and time with friends. I know quite a few people who exist like that, and sometimes they're quite happy with it. However, while you get to spend a lot of time doing what you're passionate about, down the line it can cause issues. When your whole life is revolving around one thing, it leaves little space for anything else. And if, for some reason, you have to stop that thing, even if just for a short period, you don't have much left at all. While you still spend some time with friends or finishing homework, you don't really have anything else to do. You've shaped your life around this one activity, but you haven't designed it with other interests to balance life out.

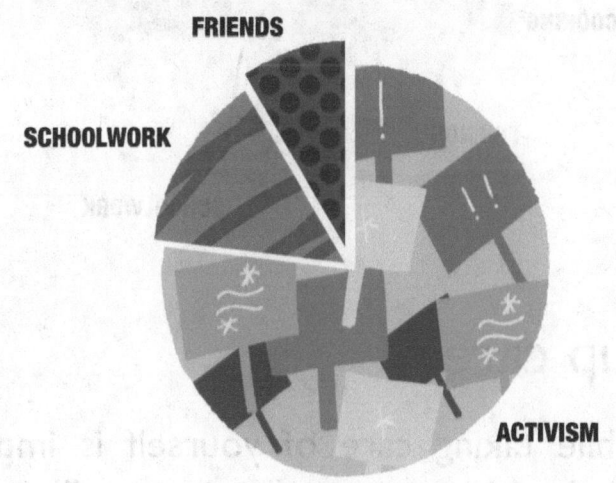

The second diagram, below, is a much better insight into what a healthy lifestyle looks like. While activism is still the largest chunk, there's time left for other things. For me, this would probably be acting, art, reading and cooking. These activities don't need to necessarily be 'productive' – rather hobbies, creative outlets and leisurely time to help you relax and be a well-rounded person. If any element is 'taken away', or you lose interest or the motivation to carry on with it, you still have plenty of interests to ensure you're doing things you enjoy.

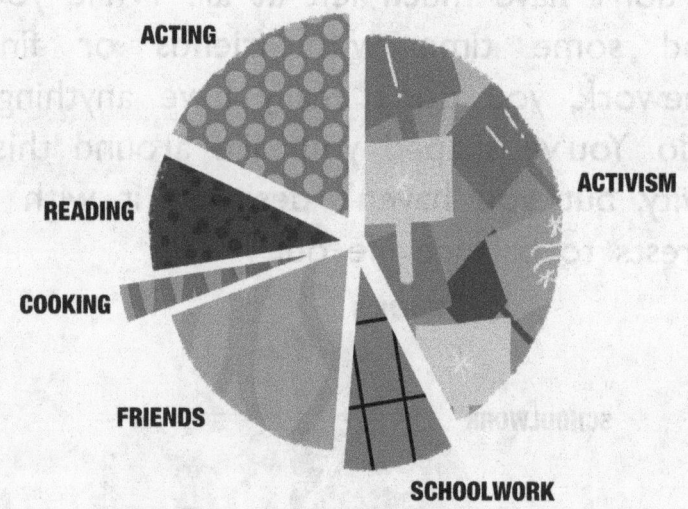

Group care

While taking care of yourself is important, to stay healthy as a collective you'll need to create systems and cultures in which you're constantly taking care of each other. When you create these systems, the responsibility of making sure you're okay isn't just placed on the individual, but the load is spread across different structures. This creates a welcoming and healthy movement, strengthening your group to make it more powerful.

The development of relationships, both internally as a group and across movements, is integral to self-care. By forming connections with others, you'll be able to work better as a team, further understand the intricacies of another person's needs and feelings, create a sense of community and prevent unnecessary conflict. Even having a small insight into another person's life, can help you understand them on a far deeper and more personal level.

Something you're unlikely to ever escape the struggle of, whether it's in activism or just generally in the world of adult employment, is understanding the difference between 'private' and 'public' relationships. A private relationship is the sort you're probably more accustomed to. This is the sort of relationship that's built on a deep and genuine connection with another person, and is intrinsically emotionally based. It's categorised by showing a side of yourself that you might not necessarily share with strangers or those you don't know very well. You show this side to those people you're close to and, because of that, trust grows between you. This is the sort of relationship you have with good friends at school, where you feel comfortable being authentically yourself and not worrying too much about the boundaries of what is and isn't okay to share.

Public relationships are more along the lines of those you'd have with teachers, for example. The sort of relationship where you understand the person and grow to know them, but there isn't a deep sense of trust or personal connection between you. This is a more surface-level understanding of someone, where you feel comfortable talking and knowing some basic information about each other's life. This might include how many siblings they have, or what they hope to study after graduating, or how their dog is doing. This sort of relationship is still important, and can give you a small but valuable insight into another person's life, so that you can check in with them and generally like each other, but you still remain professional and not particularly deeply connected. This is the sort of relationship that is more important to develop within a workspace.

While private relationships shouldn't be avoided, when a public relationship is not developed alongside it, it can cause major issues. Often, if you're good friends with someone, you don't feel as comfortable calling them out on their wrongdoings, or giving them objective and honest feedback. These private relationships can also create a sense of internal alliances and divisions in a movement, which are rarely ever healthy.

Managing group relationships

To actually develop these relationships within the group, relational meetings are necessary. While this might sound a formal and fancy term, it simply means having relaxed meetings to get to know each other better. Whether the people in your group know one another well or not, these meetings are essential for working together as a team. They're of most immediate help when you have a taskforce who haven't worked much as a group before; however, they can still have great benefits to an already comfortable working group or team. It's helpful to create a loose plan to direct the conversation, including icebreakers and check-in questions. Schedule these meetings quite frequently, somewhere between once a week and once a month.

On top of these planned relational meetings, you can add an element of connection through having introductory periods at the beginning of most meetings. This might include going around the circle and each person sharing their name, pronouns and location, in addition to answering a question or doing an activity so the group can learn something new about the individual. This might be as simple as 'What's something that made you smile today?' or more complex, such as sharing your favourite song and a memory you associate with it.

To build healthy and strong public relationships within a movement, effort needs to be placed in the right spaces. One of the best ways for this to happen is through implementing a wellbeing team. This team works to organise larger scale relational meetings, check-ins and provide a space people can reach out to for support. They also help create the policies and cultures of a healthy workplace. This might include a movie or game night, mental health support calls, task delegation systems and so on. By taking part, organisers get to know each other in a personal and light-hearted manner, allowing for growth in relationships. This also helps create a culture where everybody feels comfortable reaching out for support when they're struggling, even if not for a particularly major or important reason. What works best for you and your team might be different to what works for others – it's really a matter of trial and error to find out what best suits your style.

As a group, you should seek to develop a culture in which working to the point of exhaustion isn't idolised; rather, understanding your own limits and distributing work fairly is prioritised. It's helpful to implement different systems to ensure this is the case. For example, having personal capacity check-ins before tasks are delegated can make sure nobody is working themselves harder than they should be, and also gives a general idea of the broader workload of the movement at a given point. Additionally, everyone should feel able to alert those around them that they need a break for however long, and know that this decision will be respected and not looked down upon by fellow organisers.

The adults in the room

It can be difficult to manage how adults fit into your space. While they can be incredibly helpful mentors and invaluable to your work, it's easy to be co-opted by adult groups, or even feel that the supporters you do have are intruding into a youth space. This depends on whether you decide to have a totally youth-led group, or work with adults on the same level, and also what age limit you set for 'youth'.

Adult mentors are a very powerful resource for a young activist. While this book should hopefully provide you with all the information you need to get you on your feet, there will always be challenges unique to your situation.

Having an experienced and trusted adult activist you can reach out to will help you get past these struggles; just a quick phone call for advice can be enormously helpful. Even if you aren't facing a direct obstacle, being able to discuss strategy and viability of actions with someone who has successfully pulled off dozens of them can ensure you fine tune your ideas as much as possible. A mentor relationship might be official – with set meeting times and predetermined points of conversation – or much more casual, with someone you know you can always rely on to give good advice.

Additionally, having adults who are willing to volunteer to support you can be super useful. One of the unfortunate facts about not being a legal adult is that many bookings, forms and official processes require adults to sign them or be available at any time for a phone call (school isn't very compatible with this). Having some adults around to help out with organising and filling roles that are difficult for younger people can be incredibly valuable. If they're experienced organisers, they can help make logistical work come together, create resources for you to share and provide guidance on how to do these things.

To find adults who are willing to help, reach out to different activist groups and NGOs to see if anyone has time. Often people will be more willing to give support if you already have a relationship with them or somebody they know, so remember to think about the contacts you already have. Talk to the organisers of open activist groups to see if you could speak at a meeting to discuss what help you need and how they could get involved with your group. Adults can often seem more intimidating and difficult to approach than young people, but many would be happy to support you.

However, while having an adult in these roles can be so helpful, they should never overstep boundaries and make you or others feel intruded upon in your youth-led space. Before older people get involved, it's important to outline exactly what you want their role to be.

- Consider the importance of your group being led and directed by young people.
- Is it particularly school students or minors that should be uplifted, or generally anyone who's under twenty-something?
- For those older than your definition of 'youth', should they be involved in the decision-making processes (in particular, official votes)?
- If not, should they be able to state their opinions on sensitive manners and potentially sway people?

- Should you have exclusive youth-only spaces for planning, or are you happy for adults to be there?
- What sort of help will they be providing? Is it purely logistical, or strategic also?

Continue asking these questions and figuring out the limits you want to set for those adults helping you. Once you've made these decisions, create a code of conduct that your supporters can follow. This can vary in length, depending on the decisions made, but try to keep it concise and easily understood. When you have adults who are keen to be involved in your work, ensure that they agree to abide by any codes of conduct you have created, and that they're prepared to be held accountable. If they aren't willing to respect the limits of a youth-led space, then consider if they're the sort of people you actually want to be working with.

Many small groups that create a lot of momentum — in particular, those consisting primarily of young people — become targets for co-option by other groups. Co-option is when one (typically larger) group tries to take over another, and/or take credit for their work. When you haven't experienced situations like this before, it's easy to fall into a place where, too late, you realise that others are taking advantage of you. Before you go into any new partnership or adopt new adult mentors, question what you think their motives are, and what both of you will get out of the relationship. Does it feel that the other group has a disproportionate amount of benefits that you aren't receiving? Are they trying to take credit for, or insert themselves into, the success of your work? Do they seem to genuinely want to work on growing both movements, or do you feel that something else is going on? Do you feel that in entering this relationship your group's values will be compromised? When navigating these situations, always try to enter with an open mind. Often what you see as a red flag might be a simple misunderstanding and, if not, it will typically be something you can negotiate and get past. However, if alarm bells are ringing and you don't feel comfortable with the way you'd be working with this other group, don't be afraid to change the terms. Establish an open dialogue, make clear the issues you have, and that you still want to work together but to approach it in a different way. Be friendly and keep options open, but be firm about what you feel is crossing a line and what you are not comfortable with. If others aren't willing to discuss this relationship further and reshape the original idea, unfortunately you might have to continue separately.

At some meetings and events, as one of the few, if not only, young people in the room, you will often have others try to take advantage of you. At a summit, meeting or speaking engagement, simply being below voting age will make you a novelty. Adults love to come up and compliment you on all manner of things ... with 'for your age' slapped on the end. ('You're such an eloquent speaker for your age!' 'You're doing such amazing things for your age!' 'Can you believe they're only a teenager?'). Despite meaning well, they are implying that they expected you to speak poorly and be largely ignorant and disinterested due to the fact you haven't graduated yet. Sometimes you might feel unwelcome, or that you aren't 'qualified' enough to be there. It makes sense: such events are so different to your daily routine and can seem intimidating. Adults will often further perpetuate this by treating you differently to those older than you and generally being condescending. In those moments, remind yourself that you deserve to be in the room, and that you are equal to and as valuable as every other person present. Your age gives you a unique insight into the world, which is incredibly important and needs to be heard.

At these events, 'important' adults – usually politicians – might see you as a photo opportunity rather than someone they are willing to engage in meaningful conversation with. This can be upsetting and devaluing to you as an individual. Remember that just because someone asks to take a photo with you, it doesn't mean you have to say yes. This might seem obvious, but when you're in the moment you often feel obliged to do what's asked of you and not question it. While it might feel awkward to say no to taking a photo or filming an interview, it's important that you're able to stand your ground and not do something you're not totally comfortable with, or feel is only being done so that the older person has 'evidence' that they care about young people. In saying this, I don't mean you should never help out adults or take photos with a politician, rather that you should do this with people who you feel actually value you and the work you do and aren't there to use your image.

> **MANY PEOPLE WILL WANT TO GENUINELY ENGAGE WITH YOU AND CONTINUE DIALOGUE: YOU JUST NEED TO LEARN TO RECOGNISE THEM.**

CONCLUSION

LOOKING BACK AND LOOKING AHEAD

BEING AN ACTIVIST STILL FEELS SOMEWHAT STRANGE TO ME. It's something that has only been part of my life for a little less than three years, yet it's become one of the most defining elements of my identity. It's funny to look back on the process of writing this book, as I even feel like a completely different activist from when I started to where I stand currently. And I imagine that in another year's time, I'll look back on the girl I am now, hurriedly typing away in her bedroom at an hour when she most certainly should be asleep, and see someone almost unrecognisable. The truth is, diving headfirst into activism has been the most transformative experience of my life. It's stressful and tear-inducing at one moment, followed by pure bliss and excitement the next. Yet nothing has let me see clearer. I've learned as much about myself as I have about the world. I've come to understand the privileges I hold and the subtleties in how I navigate society, learned about the disgusting systems of injustice that govern our world and how they're near impossible to topple, yet also discovered the sheer influence and power of community and how, when people come together, just about anything is possible.

When I first took the leap of faith into change-making, I never could have imagined it would explode in the ways it has. I've experienced great wins with others along the way. There was the overwhelming vote in favour of same-sex marriage rights in the plebiscite and the achievement of marriage equality as part of the YES campaign. Then, as part of School Strike 4 Climate, I helped mobilise hundreds of thousands of Australians, achieving the support of 30 trade unions and over 3000 businesses, bringing the climate crisis to the forefront of the public conversation, above all proving that young people deserve to have a voice and will stop at nothing to ensure we're heard.

I used to spend far more time worrying about all the problems facing us today (and believe me, I'm still terrified about them). However, doing everything in my capacity to help make the world a better place has allowed me to feel a sense of calm again.

WHILE I ALONE CANNOT FIX EVERYTHING, I CAN BE A COG IN

THE ENORMOUS MACHINE THAT MAKES CHANGE HAPPEN.

As individuals we might feel powerless and insignificant, but by banding together and fighting with a united front we can completely transform our world.

I cannot urge you enough to make the choice to raise your voice. You have far more influence than you could ever imagine.

ACKNOWLEDGEMENTS

WRITING THIS BOOK HAS BEEN SUCH AN INTENSIVE PROCESS and couldn't have come to fruition without the support of an immeasurable number of people. Thank you to the entire team at Pantera for helping me every step of the way, and in particular to Lex Hirst for her invaluable guidance and encouragement from the very get go of this project. I also want to thank my Mum for her constant support and motivation, and also to the rest of my family for all their love and enthusiasm. I'm massively grateful for each and every member of School Strike 4 Climate, I have gained countless friendships and learnt so much through all my time spent with this wonderful group of people. A sincere thanks to Amanda Tattersall, for providing such insightful mentoring and advice, alongside Charlie Wood, for her tireless efforts and aid towards the SS4C movement. I'm also immensely appreciative towards all my teachers and the staff at Fort Street, for being so accommodating and supportive of the work I do. And lastly, thank you to my friends, your excitement and interest towards all of this has been so encouraging.

Jean Hinchliffe is a 17-year-old climate activist and an organiser within School Strike 4 Climate. She campaigns for legislative action against the sourcing and usage of fossil fuels, along with pushing for Australia to become fully carbon neutral.

Jean is passionate about social, political, and environmental issues and began her activism at age 13, when she volunteered with the Vote YES campaign for marriage equality. Since then, she has also volunteered with organisations such as GetUp and Stop Adani.

Lead the Way: How to change the world from a teen activist and school striker is Jean's first book.

www.ingramcontent.com/pod-product-compliance
Lightning Source LLC
Chambersburg PA
CBHW011747220426
43667CB00020B/2930